GLADYS

Staying Strong

Andrew L. Urban

Published by:
Wilkinson Publishing Pty Ltd
ACN 006 042 173
PO Box 24135
Melbourne, Vic 3001
Ph: 03 9654 5446

enquiries@wilkinsonpublishing.com.au
www.wilkinsonpublishing.com.au

Title: Gladys Staying Strong

ISBN: 9781922810199

eBook ISBN: 9781922810953

A catalogue record of this book is available from the National Library of Australia.

Design by Spike Creative Pty Ltd
Ph: (03) 9427 9500
spikecreative.com.au

Printed and bound in Australia by Griffin Press

CONTENTS

AUTHOR'S NOTE

I've been writing about wrongful convictions in the criminal justice system since 2013. The central concern in that troubled area is the role of the State in its fair and just administration of the law. You will have already surmised that for me, the matter of how the institutions tasked with safeguarding public service integrity falls within that same socio-political and legal framework.

As with the criminal justice system, the apprehension and prosecution of criminals is a benefit to society that we all applaud. But also as with the criminal justice system, we abhor convicting the innocent. The well know formulation attributed to 18th century English jurist William Blackstone comes to mind: It is better that ten guilty persons go free than one innocent suffer.

Unlike criminal courts, the NSW Independent Commission Against Corruption (ICAC) does not provide the protections offered those charged with a crime, nor the exoneration process that an acquittal or successful appeal offers. Hence, guilt of corrupt behaviour by accusation is a real and constant danger, as history shows. (See ICAC – a damaged history)

Wrongful accusation delivers a grave injustice and in the case of a corruption 'watchdog' a public investigation amounts to a wrongful accusation, given that the investigation is not a finding.

I make these points to explain my interest in the story of Gladys Berejiklian; it goes to justice and how agencies of the state must be the protectors of citizens, not a predator.

In order to fully demonstrate how 'Gladys was done over', in Prime Minister Scott Morrison's words, this book contains detailed excerpts from the ICAC Act and from the public investigation that was broadcast live – much of which I watched. The transcript excerpts are revealing of course, but they don't capture the body language, facial expressions and general demeanour of the participants. (Nor do they reflect the abysmal quality of the live stream footage.)

Some of the exchanges published in this book demonstrate how contrary to natural justice that process can be. But of course, anything is permissible in the pursuit of political corruption, right? The end justifies the means, right? Wrong and wrong, in my view.

Reading the exact wording of questions posed by Counsel Assisting doesn't convey the often smug and argumentative tone. My intention is to provide the broader context in which this controversial ICAC investigation pilloried Gladys Berijiklian with questionable justification – and arguably not in the true spirit of exposing political corruption as the public understands it.

FOREWORD

In 2003, my son Chris Wyllie had the honour to be the Captain of Willoughby Public School. His role included welcoming the new local Member for the State seat of Willoughby. The night before we practised, slowly, syllable by syllable, the correct pronunciation of "Ms Gladys Berejiklian".

The introduction was fluent and the response, from the lady herself, was gracious and warm. In the 2011 election, when the Liberal Party defeated the 16 year incumbent opposition in a landslide, Chris and his classmates had the opportunity to cast the first electoral votes of their lives for Gladys, as everyone in her electorate knew her by then.

There was never a local Member for Willoughby as approachable as Gladys. She is natural. She is modest. She has an enthusiasm which is infectious. She is good-humoured. She is just a lovely woman. A woman who never complained that she had been in any way disadvantaged by her gender. She had no doubt been fortified by real challenges like starting school in Sydney at 5 being unable to speak any English. She excelled at school and developed great mastery of both English and her parents' language, Armenian.

I came to know Gladys too and when, as Premier, she was my ultimate boss in the closing years of the 42 I spent in the service of New South Wales, she was enormously supportive. In 2019, after I had commenced private practice, I was buying a sushi lunch in a city food hall. From behind I heard a particularly cheery: "Hi Margaret". I turned and said: "Hello Premier" and she shook my hand and enquired about how I was faring. She is genuinely interested in, and committed to, the service of others. She is eminently likeable.

But, as Lavrentiy Beria, one of Stalin's secret police chiefs, boasted: "Show me the man and I'll show you the crime". ICAC, the investigatory body which destroyed the political careers of former Liberal Premiers Nick Greiner and Barry O'Farrell (both since exonerated) came after a particularly popular Premier, and one who had led her State through perhaps the most successful response to the Covid breakout that the World was to see. Late in 2021, just weeks before Premier Berejiklian planned to free her State's people from Covid depredations, ICAC summonsed her to public hearings about her relationship with an allegedly corrupt member of parliament. Regardless of the fact that private hearings into the same matters had already been held, ICAC decided its inquiry was too urgent to wait for the Premier to lead her State out of lockdown. Ms Berejiklian realised she could not continue as Premier while she was subjected to public and prurient interrogation about her private life.

Yet, as this Foreword is written, more than 6 months after the conclusion of the hearings, there is no result for Gladys Berejiklian, who is now in a senior executive role at Optus. We all wish her well. The people of New South Wales were robbed of a democratically elected Premier who, regardless of what might ever be recommended by ICAC, will never be considered a "corrupt" person.

It is rare for someone of the qualities of Gladys Berejiklian – intelligent, industrious, diligent and dedicated to service – to offer him or herself to public life. In addition she is the child of immigrants for whom English is a second language, and a woman. Her record was exemplary and unblemished.

Still she was cut down by the ICAC, which is yet to tell us why*. I predict that she, like her predecessors, will eventually be totally exonerated. I live in hope that the ICAC will finally be held to account by a Government courageous enough to do so.

MARGARET CUNNEEN SC

*July 13, 2022

DONE OVER

" ... the people of NSW know that the former Premier was done over..."
Prime Minister Scott Morrison in parliament, November 25, 2021.

PM BLASTS 'KANGAROO COURT' ICAC MODEL
Sky News Afternoon Agenda, November 25, 2021

Well before the ICAC announced any of its findings in Operation Keppel investigating former MP Daryl Maguire – and by extension his former girlfriend now former Premier Gladys Berejiklian - a month or so after public hearings concluded, Graham Richardson's column in The Australian of November 26, 2021, was headlined *'In hi-tech era, no evading long arm of the law'*, illustrated in the digital edition with a large photo of Berejiklian taken at the ICAC inquiry.

He begins: "It is hard to imagine a body like the NSW Independent Commission Against Corruption being set up in America, the land of the free and the home of the brave, where freedom for the individual is valued at a far higher price than here in Australia. In an era where technology enables law enforcement bodies ready access to all kinds of financial records, miscreants eventually are all caught."

He recalls how "As minister for social security I saw first hand what the matching of banking records could do. Some people got away with claiming a disability pension and unemployment benefits for many years, but all of them were discovered eventually. Many spent years paying back their ill-gotten gains, while others less fortunate became guests of Her Majesty for quite a few years.

"The higher the benefits available, the higher the motivation to defraud the public purse. Australia and Britain have the most generous social security systems in the world and for some the temptation to cheat is too hard to resist. The checks and balances available to government mean cheating is only for mugs.

"When there is a certainty about being caught, only a mug would continue their nefarious activities. Given the numbers being caught, the rewards would have to be pretty good."

Then he discusses how "For many years people arrived in Australia from Vietnam after travelling in leaky boats across potentially dangerous waters. The reward was worth the risk. The trip from Libya or any other war-torn hellhole in Africa must be worth the risk. Mothers take their children on these extremely hazardous journeys, and that is the measure of what they are escaping and the place they are heading for.

"Sadly, the sight of bodies floating on the Mediterranean has become far too common. Many of those leaving North Africa and claiming refugee status in Europe or Britain are, in fact, economic refugees seeking a better life.

"It is not too hard to imagine that over time the numbers seeking to abandon hopelessness in Africa and find security, both economic and personal, in Europe will continue to grow, and grow quickly."

He concludes by observing that "Customs officials earning less than $100,000 a year can be offered that much just for turning their head the other way at the right moment on just one night. Those mathematics guarantee a long and happy life for the drug trade.

"I have long been an advocate for legalising drug-taking and of making the purchase of drugs a payment to the government. It is the government that should run this wretched trade.

"Corruption is getting easier to find and stand out as technology develops.

"The one thing you can't hide is cash, as the discovery of millions of dollars stashed in the roof of the home of one notorious family member has shown. Better the government be the recipient of those millions and have them used for community benefit."

That's it. There is no mention of Berijiklian in his column, despite what the photo below the headline suggests.

There, in a nutshell, the effect of being investigated by the ICAC is revealed. The fear that the ICAC smear is like the blood that won't wash off Lady Macbeth's hands is well founded – although not always so rightly (wrongly?) earned.

It wasn't Richo who chose the photo or wrote the headline; it was a nameless sub-editor, a once respected participant of newspaper publishing (fact and spell checker, and sub-editor in the literal sense), the equivalent of the once respected public servant who could be relied upon to work quietly, professionally and without an agenda. Excuse the nostalgia.

That she was effectively defamed by the juxtaposing of headline/photo is unquestionable. It is also unquestionable that the mindset at work connected Richo's column – however loosely – with the ICAC's investigation of Berejiklian. Investigation is perhaps the wrong word for the process; we'll get to that later. What more suitable bedfellows than the faceless subterranean manipulators within the media and the faceless operators of the ICAC's domain? More on that later, too.

There is no legal recourse for Berejiklian in the real courts of justice. Nor is this the only instance where an appearance at the ICAC promotes an appearance of corruption. That, of course, is the principal complaint levelled at the ICAC over the years. There's a question: why "over the years"? When a vehicle is found not fit for purpose – its wheels unaligned, its engine over-revving, its windscreen covered in dirt – it is subjected to a full maintenance service, where mechanics go through a check list of deficiencies to mend. It doesn't, or shouldn't, take years to book it in.

In the very same November 26, 2021 edition of The Australian, Legal Affairs Correspondent and Vice President of the Rule of Law Institute, Chris Merritt, made the point that "Berejiklian is before ICAC not because she stands accused of providing an unlawful pecuniary benefit for herself or Maguire – she is there because the NSW parliament decided years ago to twist the meaning of the word "corruption" so a substantial breach of the ministerial code is, for the purposes of the ICAC Act, corruption.

"This, to use a technical term, is madness.

"If Berejiklian is found corrupt, it will mean that a substantial breach of the code – without any allegation of financial wrongdoing – can generate exactly the same finding that was handed to Eddie Obeid.

"Berejiklian was wrong about not disclosing her relationship with Maguire.

"That is a breach of a political document – the ministerial code – and should have resulted in a political penalty ... not an elaborate show trial at taxpayers' expense."

Merritt points to the flawed decision by the NSW parliament to twist the definition of corruption for the purposes of the ICAC Act. But then the NSW parliament under Mike Baird had already retro-fitted the ICAC to make some previously illegal actions legal. Why?

For an agency with oversight of public officers' integrity, it seems to have had trouble with the notion of integrity itself.

For example: The Australian's Sharri Markson reported on October 22, 2015, how "The agency re-enacted a seizure of Margaret Cunneen SC's mobile phone from her home (*on July 30, 2014*) in order to cover-up a flawed raid a week earlier when they took her phone without a search warrant. ICAC allegedly obtained a search warrant to seize a mobile phone from Ms Cunneen's home that was already in its possession.

"When ICAC first took Ms Cunneen's mobile phone, officers used a "notice to produce" request. A "notice to produce" ordinarily requires someone to attend ICAC's offices and produce certain documents.

"It is alleged the officers visited Ms Cunneen's home a week later, this time with a search warrant, to simulate a lawful seizure of the mobile phone. It is understood that one of the officers held the phone while another switched on a video-camera and recorded taking the mobile phone."

Then ICAC Commissioner, Megan Latham, infamously quipped to law students that they might enjoy work at ICAC because it was like tearing wings off butterflies, revealing an inappropriate corporate culture that has been confirmed by subsequent behaviour.

Why is working at ICAC like tearing wings off butterflies? This short Chris Merritt-inspired list of rhetorical questions is helpful: Is it because ICAC tends to ignore the rules of evidence and bases its decisions on material that would never pass muster in a court? Is it because ICAC enjoys special status so the merits of its findings can never be tested on appeal? Or is it because defence counsel cannot test the credibility of prosecution witnesses in cross examination, unless the commission, which presents those witnesses, agrees.

In December 2018, Morgan Begg of the Institute of Public Affairs echoed Prime Minister Morrison – or was it the other way round – when he wrote: "Wide-ranging anti-corruption agencies too often turn into kangaroo courts. Tackling corruption is on its face a highly virtuous mission, and agencies committed to this are always under threat of elevating this mission above inconveniences such as complying with the rule of law and respecting the legal rights of individuals caught up in their investigations.

"In NSW, the Independent Commission Against Corruption has left a trail of destruction in its wake since its establishment in 1988. It has proven much better at destroying lives and careers than it has at tackling real criminality.

"Its pursuit of Australian Water Holdings in 2014 ended the political career of then premier Barry O'Farrell for failing to remember receiving a bottle of wine.

"A magistrate in 2016 dismissed allegations of misconduct against former emergency services commissioner Murray Kear from an incident in 2013.

"ICAC also has displayed a tendency to exceed its defined authority, as the High Court found in the commission's pursuits of former NSW premier Nick Greiner in 1994 and former crown prosecutor Margaret Cunneen in 2015." (Does exceeding its authority constitute corrupt conduct? See s 8 of the Act below, especially perhaps 2a. No, it constitutes abuse of power.)

Begg, Director, Legal Rights Program at the Institute of Public Affairs, makes the point that "the incentive for politicians is never to criticise ICAC lest they be criticised as weak on corruption. When the High Court in 2015 ruled the NSW ICAC had gone too far with its powers, the state rewarded ICAC with retrospective statutory validation for past investigations."

So the government of former premier Mike Baird thus took away the right to a legal remedy for all those who had been harmed by ICAC's mistakes. "The most regrettable part of this affair is that the government sided with an agency that had engaged in unlawful conduct," wrote Chris Merritt.

The NSW parliament recklessly ignored the red alert lights on the ICAC dashboard and failed to book it in for service for hubris damage that was so obviously needed. Berejiklian herself could have 'booked it in' to reverse Baird's unforgivable legislation. She might be wishing that she had …

THE ACT

Considering the reliance on the Act that governs ICAC, I believe it is valuable to have some of the relevant sections of the Act available as a reference. In some instances, Counsel Assisting cites sections for validation – interpretations with which some readers (and the author) might disagree.

Independent Commission Against Corruption Act 1988 No 35 (as at 1/7/2021)

(The following extracts exclude elements that are not relevant to the subject of this book. All the same, it is an opportunity for the public to examine the source of the ICAC's powers.)

7 Corrupt conduct

(1) For the purposes of this Act, corrupt conduct is any conduct which falls within the description of corrupt conduct in section 8, but which is not excluded by section 9.

(2) Conduct comprising a conspiracy or attempt to commit or engage in conduct that would be corrupt conduct under section 8 shall itself be regarded as corrupt conduct under section 8.

(3) Conduct comprising such a conspiracy or attempt is not excluded by section 9 if, had the conspiracy or attempt been brought to fruition in further conduct, the further conduct could constitute or involve an offence or grounds referred to in that section.

8 General nature of corrupt conduct

(1) Corrupt conduct is—

(a) any conduct of any person (whether or not a public official) that adversely affects, or that could adversely affect, either directly or indirectly, the honest or impartial exercise of official functions by any public official, any group or body of public officials or any public authority, or

(b) any conduct of a public official that constitutes or involves the dishonest or partial exercise of any of his or her official functions, or

(c) any conduct of a public official or former public official that constitutes or involves a breach of public trust, or

(d) any conduct of a public official or former public official that involves the misuse of information or material that he or she has acquired in the course of his or her official functions, whether or not for his or her benefit or for the benefit of any other person.

(2) Corrupt conduct is also any conduct of any person (whether or not a public official) that adversely affects, or that could adversely affect, either directly or indirectly, the exercise of official functions by any public official, any group or body of public officials or any public authority and which could involve any of the following matters—

(a) official misconduct (including breach of trust, fraud in office, nonfeasance, misfeasance, malfeasance, oppression, extortion or imposition),

(b) bribery,

(c) blackmail,

(d) obtaining or offering secret commissions,

(e) fraud,

(f) theft,

(g) perverting the course of justice,

(h) embezzlement,

(i) election bribery,

(j) election funding offences,

(k) election fraud,

(l) treating (*ie election fraud*),

(m) tax evasion,

(n) revenue evasion,
(o) currency violations,
(p) illegal drug dealings,
(q) illegal gambling,
(r) obtaining financial benefit by vice engaged in by others,
(s) bankruptcy and company violations,
(t) harbouring criminals,
(u) forgery,
(v) treason or other offences against the Sovereign,
(w) homicide or violence,
(x) matters of the same or a similar nature to any listed above,
(y) any conspiracy or attempt in relation to any of the above.

(2A) Corrupt conduct is also any conduct of any person (whether or not a public official) that impairs, or that could impair, public confidence in public administration and which could involve any of the following matters—

(a) collusive tendering,
(b) fraud in relation to applications for licences, permits or other authorities under legislation designed to protect health and safety or the environment or designed to facilitate the management and commercial exploitation of resources,
(c) dishonestly obtaining or assisting in obtaining, or dishonestly benefiting from, the payment or application of public funds for private advantage or the disposition of public assets for private advantage,
(d) defrauding the public revenue,
(e) fraudulently obtaining or retaining employment or appointment as a public official.

(3) Conduct may amount to corrupt conduct under subsection (1), (2) or (2A) even though it occurred before the

commencement of that subsection, and it does not matter that some or all of the effects or other ingredients necessary to establish such corrupt conduct occurred before that commencement and that any person or persons involved are no longer public officials.

(4) Conduct committed by or in relation to a person who was not or is not a public official may amount to corrupt conduct under this section with respect to the exercise of his or her official functions after becoming a public official. This subsection extends to a person seeking to become a public official even if the person fails to become a public official.

(5) Conduct may amount to corrupt conduct under this section even though it occurred outside the State or outside Australia, and matters listed in subsection (2) or (2A) refer to—

(a) matters arising in the State or matters arising under the law of the State, or

(b) matters arising outside the State or outside Australia or matters arising under the law of the Commonwealth or under any other law.

(6) The specific mention of a kind of conduct in a provision of this section shall not be regarded as limiting or expanding the scope of any other provision of this section.

9 Limitation on nature of corrupt conduct

(1) Despite section 8, conduct does not amount to corrupt conduct unless it could constitute or involve—

(a) a criminal offence, or

(b) a disciplinary offence, or

(c) reasonable grounds for dismissing, dispensing with the

services of or otherwise terminating the services of a public official, or

(d) in the case of conduct of a Minister of the Crown or a member of a House of Parliament—a substantial breach of an applicable code of conduct.

(2) It does not matter that proceedings or action for such an offence can no longer be brought or continued, or that action for such dismissal, dispensing or other termination can no longer be taken.

(3) For the purposes of this section—

applicable code of conduct means, in relation to—

(a) a Minister of the Crown—a ministerial code of conduct prescribed or adopted for the purposes of this section by the regulations, or

(b) a member of the Legislative Council or of the Legislative Assembly (including a Minister of the Crown)—a code of conduct adopted for the purposes of this section by resolution of the House concerned.

criminal offence means a criminal offence under the law of the State or under any other law relevant to the conduct in question.

disciplinary offence includes any misconduct, irregularity, neglect of duty, breach of discipline or other matter that constitutes or may constitute grounds for disciplinary action under any law.

(4) Subject to subsection (5), conduct of a Minister of the Crown or a member of a House of Parliament which falls within the description of corrupt conduct in section 8 is not excluded by this section if it is conduct that would cause a reasonable person to believe that it would bring the integrity of the office concerned or of Parliament into serious disrepute.

(5) Without otherwise limiting the matters that it can under section 74A (1) include in a report under section 74, the Commission is not authorised to include a finding or opinion that a specified person has, by engaging in conduct of a kind referred to in subsection (4), engaged in corrupt conduct, unless the Commission is satisfied that the conduct constitutes a breach of a law (apart from this Act) and the Commission identifies that law in the report.

(6) A reference to a disciplinary offence in this section and sections 74A and 74B includes a reference to a substantial breach of an applicable requirement of a code of conduct required to be complied with under section 440 (5) of the Local Government Act 1993 but does not include a reference to any other breach of such a requirement.

10 Complaints about possible corrupt conduct

(1) Any person may make a complaint to the Commission about a matter that concerns or may concern corrupt conduct.

(2) The Commission may investigate a complaint or decide that a complaint need not be investigated.

(3) The Commission may discontinue an investigation of a complaint.

(4) If a prisoner informs the governor of the prison that the prisoner wishes to make a complaint under this section, the governor of the prison must—

(a) take all steps necessary to facilitate the making of the complaint, and

(b) send immediately to the Commission, unopened, any written matter addressed to the Commission.

(5) For the purposes of subsection (4), ***prisoner*** and ***governor of a prison*** have the same meanings as ***inmate*** and ***governor*** have in the *Crimes (Administration of Sentences) Act 1999.*

11 Duty to notify Commission of possible corrupt conduct

(1) This section applies to the following persons—

(a) the Ombudsman,

(b) the Commissioner of Police,

(c) the principal officer of a public authority,

(d) an officer who constitutes a public authority,

(e) a Minister of the Crown.

(2) A person to whom this section applies is under a duty to report to the Commission any matter that the person suspects on reasonable grounds concerns or may concern corrupt conduct.

(2A) Despite subsection (2), the Commissioner of Police is not under a duty to report to the Commission any matter that concerns or may concern corrupt conduct of a police officer or administrative employee (within the meaning of the *Law Enforcement Conduct Commission Act 2016*) unless the Commissioner of Police suspects on reasonable grounds that the matter also concerns or may concern corrupt conduct of another public official.

(2B) Despite subsection (2), the Commissioner for the New South Wales Crime Commission (***the Crime Commissioner***) is not under a duty to report to the Commission any matter that concerns or may concern corrupt conduct of a Crime Commission officer (within the meaning of the *Law Enforcement Conduct Commission Act 2016*) unless the Crime Commissioner suspects on reasonable grounds that the matter also concerns or may concern corrupt conduct of another public official.

(3) The Commission may issue guidelines as to what matters need or need not be reported.

(3A) A Minister of the Crown who is under a duty under this section to report a matter may (despite subsection (2)) report the matter either to the Commission or to the head of any agency responsible to the Minister.

(4) This section has effect despite any duty of secrecy or other restriction on disclosure.

(5) The regulations may prescribe who is the principal officer of a public authority, but in the absence of regulations applying in relation to a particular public authority, the principal officer is the person who is the head of the authority, its most senior officer or the person normally entitled to preside at its meetings.

(6) The regulations may prescribe the principal officer of a separate office within a public authority as the principal officer of the public authority in relation to matters concerning the separate office.

***

21 Power to obtain information

(1) For the purposes of an investigation, the Commission may, by notice in writing served on a public authority or public official, require the authority or official to produce a statement of information.

(2) A notice under this section must specify or describe the information concerned, must fix a time and date for compliance and must specify the person (being a Commissioner, an Assistant Commissioner or any other officer of the Commission) to whom the production is to be made.

(3) The notice may provide that the requirement may be satisfied by some other person acting on behalf of the public authority

or public official and may, but need not, specify the person or class of persons who may so act.

22 Power to obtain documents etc

(1) For the purposes of an investigation, the Commission may, by notice in writing served on a person (whether or not a public authority or public official), require the person—

(a) to attend, at a time and place specified in the notice, before a person (being a Commissioner, an Assistant Commissioner or any other officer of the Commission) specified in the notice, and

(b) to produce at that time and place to the person so specified a document or other thing specified in the notice.

(2) The notice may provide that the requirement may be satisfied by some other person acting on behalf of the person on whom it was imposed and may, but need not, specify the person or class of persons who may so act.

23 Power to enter public premises

(1) For the purposes of an investigation, a Commissioner or an officer of the Commission authorised in writing by a Commissioner may, at any time—

(a) enter and inspect any premises occupied or used by a public authority or public official in that capacity, and

(b) inspect any document or other thing in or on the premises, and

(c) take copies of any document in or on the premises.

(2) (Repealed)

(3) The public authority or public official shall make available to a Commissioner or authorised officer such facilities as are

necessary to enable the powers conferred by this section to be exercised.

24 Privilege as regards information, documents etc

(1) This section applies where, under section 21 or 22, the Commission requires any person—

(a) to produce any statement of information, or

(b) to produce any document or other thing.

(2) The Commission shall set aside the requirement if it appears to the Commission that any person has a ground of privilege whereby, in proceedings in a court of law, the person might resist a like requirement and it does not appear to the Commission that the person consents to compliance with the requirement.

(3) The person must however comply with the requirement despite—

(a) any rule which in proceedings in a court of law might justify an objection to compliance with a like requirement on grounds of public interest, or

(b) any privilege of a public authority or public official in that capacity which the authority or official could have claimed in a court of law, or

(c) any duty of secrecy or other restriction on disclosure applying to a public authority or public official or a former public authority or public official.

25 Privilege as regards entry on public premises

(1) This section applies to the powers of entry, inspection and copying conferred by section 23.

(2) The powers shall not be exercised if it appears to a

Commissioner or authorised officer that any person has a ground of privilege whereby, in proceedings in a court of law, the person might resist inspection of the premises or production of the document or other thing and it does not appear to the Commissioner or authorised officer that the person consents to the inspection or production.

(3) The powers may however be exercised despite—

(a) any rule of law which, in proceedings in a court of law, might justify an objection to an inspection of the premises or to production of the document or other thing on grounds of public interest, or

(b) any privilege of a public authority or public official in that capacity which the authority or official could have claimed in a court of law, or

(c) any duty of secrecy or other restriction on disclosure applying to a public authority or public official.

26 Self-incrimination

(1) This section applies where, under section 21 or 22, the Commission requires any person—

(a) to produce any statement of information, or

(b) to produce any document or other thing.

(2) If the statement, document or other thing tends to incriminate the person and the person objects to production at the time, neither the fact of the requirement nor the statement, document or thing itself (if produced) may be used in any proceedings against the person (except proceedings for an offence against this Act or except as provided by section 114A (5)).

(3) They may however be used for the purposes of the investigation concerned, despite any such objection.

***

30 Compulsory examinations

(1) For the purposes of an investigation, the Commission may, if it is satisfied that it is in the public interest to do so, conduct a compulsory examination.

(2) A compulsory examination is to be conducted by a Commissioner or by an Assistant Commissioner, as determined by a Commissioner.

(3) A person required to attend a compulsory examination is entitled to be informed, before or at the commencement of the compulsory examination, of the nature of the allegation or complaint being investigated.

(4) A failure to comply with subsection (3) does not invalidate or otherwise affect the compulsory examination.

(5) A compulsory examination is to be conducted in private.

Note—

Section 17 (2) requires the Commission to conduct compulsory examinations with as little emphasis on an adversarial approach as possible.

(6) The Commission may (but is not required to) advise a person required to attend a compulsory examination of any findings it has made or opinions it has formed as a result of the compulsory examination.

31 Public inquiries

(1) For the purposes of an investigation, the Commission may, if it is satisfied that it is in the public interest to do so, conduct a public inquiry.

(2) Without limiting the factors that it may take into account in determining whether or not it is in the public interest to

conduct a public inquiry, the Commission is to consider the following—

(a) the benefit of exposing to the public, and making it aware, of corrupt conduct,

(b) the seriousness of the allegation or complaint being investigated,

(c) any risk of undue prejudice to a person's reputation (including prejudice that might arise from not holding an inquiry),

(d) whether the public interest in exposing the matter is outweighed by the public interest in preserving the privacy of the persons concerned.

The spirit of Section 31, above, is of particular relevance in this investigation as it relates to Gladys Berejiklian. It is arguable that, as Chris Merritt points out, hers is "a breach of a political document – the ministerial code – and should have resulted in a political penalty ... not an elaborate show trial at taxpayers' expense."

The biggest issue, perhaps, is the vague definition of corruption used by ICAC in NSW. This has been highlighted by John Nicholson, a former acting inspector of ICAC, who has written that the definition of corruption in that state permits the commission to use "an uncertain standard".

If the definition of corruption is vague, so is the boundary of the commission's jurisdiction.

In other words, the corruption case against Berejiklian is a 'false positive'; it may appear to be valid but is not. The following pages are in support of that argument. Taken together with its damaged history, the entire apparatus of ICAC appears as vindictive, shallow and – ironically enough - sometimes lacking integrity. Certainly not fit for purpose – at least not the purpose intended.

That view is shared by the veteran political commentator, Paul Kelly, The Australian's Editor-at-Large. Writing (on December 1, 2021) about the risks for the government in a national integrity commission debate, he is scathing about "the abuses of power that mark the NSW Independent Commission Against Corruption." It is worth quoting him at length in the context of this book:

"The Liberal Party has nobody but itself to blame for the troubles it faces over this issue. Coalition governments in NSW have entrenched in law an ICAC model repeatedly shown to have major flaws. The NSW Liberal Party finds itself in the situation where it has ownership of a model that has destroyed three Liberal premiers and embodies a serious governance defect – giving an outside body power to make findings on the ministerial code of conduct.

"This is pure folly. Any translation of this model to national politics would have far-reaching consequences. ICAC's defects would be magnified enormously at the national level where allegations of corruption are now a standard political tactic. The combination of ICAC's power with the act's vague definition of corruption would constitute a new avenue for continuation of political warfare.

"The Prime Minister said he wanted an integrity commission focused on criminal conduct. But this won't be easy to achieve. Consider the ICAC Act, where you find that corrupt conduct is, among other things, about "a breach of public trust". How wide is this? We know what fraud is – but breaches of public trust enter the realm of the selective and subjective. The act says conduct can be corrupt that "could" adversely affect the impartial exercise of official functions.

"Can you imagine losing two prime ministers, neither of whom was actually corrupt – the parallels being Nick Greiner and Barry O'Farrell? Can you imagine how an outside body – in effect, a standing royal commission – would have the power to arbitrate on ministerial responsibility under the statutory cover of generous definitions of corruption? Can you imagine any prime minister, Liberal or Labor, being stupid enough to devise a ministerial code and then handing power of finding to an outside body?

"I think not. At some point in the future when the national parliament legislates a national integrity commission it will have the advantage of drawing on the immense defects of the NSW model.

"The ICAC model enshrines public inquiries as an instrument of deterrence. These are authorised show trials, a design feature supposedly in the public interest.

"The effect is lethal – the official involved is discredited or terminated even before an ICAC finding. You are doomed at appearance. This is supposed to be fair and balanced? The model, moreover, is tied to the imitation of judicial proceedings.

"A 2017 parliamentary inquiry was told by John Nicholson SC, then acting inspector, Office of the Inspector of ICAC, that "everybody bows to the commissioner when he or she comes in, witnesses are called and it is in a room which is clearly set up like a courtroom. It is very difficult to avoid telescoping one into the other."

"Much of the public sees the ICAC process as akin to a court. There is a convenient alignment between ICAC and the media – a classic in mutual institutional self-interest on vivid display in the Gladys Berejiklian case.

"ICAC can begin an investigation on its own initiative or on a complaint, report or reference made to it. ICAC can consider any factor it thinks fit in deciding whether to investigate, including if a complaint is vexatious or trivial."

He says a federal commission along ICAC lines would "underline … the corruption tactic."

"… the NSW record again highlights the problem – seen in its investigation of former prosecutor Margaret Cunneen, an issue that went to the High Court where a majority found ICAC had exceeded its proper remit. ICAC's abuse of its powers over Cunneen proved the guardians are not beyond reproach."

And he makes the point that "The NSW model at the national level would become a focus of polarised politics and institutional rivalry. The remedy would be worse than the problem. The country, sadly, has tired of discussing reform and finds discussing corruption more satisfying."

The basis for the ICAC investigation:

"The ICAC is investigating allegations that, from 2012 to August 2018, the then NSW Member of Parliament for Wagga Wagga, Mr Daryl Maguire, engaged in conduct that involved a breach of public trust by using his public office, involving his duties as a member of the NSW Parliament, and the use of parliamentary resources, to improperly gain a benefit for himself and/or entities close to him. These entities included G8wayinternational/ G8wayinternational Pty Ltd and associated persons."

– ICAC official statement.

Public hearings before THE HONOURABLE RUTH McCOLL AO SC COMMISSIONER.

This further public inquiry followed additional investigative steps – not revealed - that were taken since the adjournment of the first public inquiry conducted in September and October 2020.

"After the First Public Inquiry was adjourned and having regard to the evidence received in that public inquiry, the Commission decided that it was in the public interest for Operation Keppel to be expanded so as to include an investigation into certain allegations concerning the Honourable Gladys Berejiklian. To date, that expanded investigation has been performed in private including through the use of this Commission's powers to require production of documents and statements of information and through the conduct of (private) compulsory examinations."

Counsel Assisting, Scott Robertson, goes on to explain how the ICAC Act was amended in 1995, by the NSW Government "to prescribe for the purposes of the ICAC Act an 'applicable code of conduct' in relation to Ministers of the Crown.

That was an amendment that twisted the meaning of the word "corruption" so a substantial breach of the ministerial code was included in the definitions.

That is the 'twist' to which Chris Merritt referred in his November 26, 2021 column in The Australian (see earlier).

You might find it ironic that "The presently 'applicable code of conduct' for Ministers of the Crown is the one prescribed on the advice of the Berejiklian Government on 1 September 2017."

It is instructive to see in detail how Mr Robertson, Counsel Assisting framed the second public inquiry. Note in particular how paragraphs 18 & 22 imply (by inclusion) a breach by Berejiklian which is not actually alleged; it is a conflation that serves only to smear her at the start of this public hearing.

From the Opening Statement of Counsel Assisting the Commission, Scott Robertson and Alex Brown, 18 October, 2021:

18. The Berejiklian Ministerial Code of Conduct is in substantially the same form as the Baird Ministerial Code of Conduct save that the Berejiklian Code of Conduct was amended late last year so as expressly to prohibit Ministers and Parliamentary Secretaries from accepting or seeking payment of a commission from a property developer, either directly or through a third party.
19. The Berejiklian Ministerial Code of Conduct commences by

observing that: It is essential to the maintenance of public confidence in the integrity of Government that Ministers exhibit and be seen to exhibit the highest standards of probity in the exercise of their offices and that they pursue and be seen to pursue the best interests of the people of New South Wales to the exclusion of any other interest.

20. To further those principles, the Code of Conduct "prescribes standards of ethical behaviour and imposes internal governance practices directed towards ensuring that possible breaches of ethical standards are avoided".
21. For example, cl 6 of the Code expressly provides that: A Minister, in the exercise or performance of their official functions, must not act dishonestly, must act only in what they consider to be the public interest, and must not act improperly for their private benefit or for the private benefit of any other person.
22. Further, clause 7, subclause (1) of the Code provides that: A Minister must not knowingly conceal a conflict of interest from the Premier. And clause 7, subclause (2) provides that: A Minister must not, without the written approval of the Premier, make or participate in the making of any decision or take any other action in relation to a matter in which the Minister is aware they have a conflict of interest.

Counsel Assisting went on: "A conflict of interest arises in relation to a Minister if there is a conflict between the public duty and the private interest of the Minister, in which the Minister's private interest could objectively have the potential to influence the performance of their public duty.

"The kinds of interests that may be "private interests" for the purposes of the Code are manifold and include what could be described as private concerns or personal connections. For example, where a Minister's attention or concern is particularly engaged in relation to a person by reason of their personal association or connection with them – whether that association or connection be one of friendship, enmity, family relation or romantic involvement – a "private interest" for the purposes of the Code may exist depending upon the circumstances. That explains why it is sometimes necessary (and, in many cases, will at least be desirable) for a Minister to disclose any substantial personal connection that she or he has to a person relevant to a proposed decision, even if the Minister would not her or himself receive a private benefit if the decision is made."

Mr Robertson then gave examples of how

(a) in 2013, Ms Berejiklian declared an interest to Cabinet and abstained from discussions regarding the appointment of a particular individual to a government board "due to attendance with [that individual] at functions";

(b) in 2017, Ms Berejiklian made a disclosure under the NSW Ministerial Code of Conduct to the effect that two of her cousins were then employed in the NSW Public Service;

c) in 2018, Ms Berejiklian made a declaration of interest to Cabinet in relation to a particular Liberal Party supporter in relation to a potential appointment of that person to a Government advisory board; and

(d) in 2019, Ms Berejiklian declared to Cabinet that a particular person proposed to be appointed to a government board was "known to [her]".

In other words, counsel was explaining how diligently Ms Berejiklian had always complied with the Ministerial code of conduct.

"So far as the material presently available to this Commission reveals, Ms Berejiklian never gave a disclosure under the NSW Ministerial Code of Conduct in relation to Mr Maguire.

"The foregoing is not to suggest that a "conflict of interest" for the purposes of the Code will always exist whenever a Minister has a substantial personal connection to a person associated with a particular decision or other action. Indeed, the NSW Ministerial Code of Conduct itself recognises that some substantial personal connections might not raise a conflict of interest but nevertheless permits a Minister to, in her or his discretion, disclose an interest and abstain from decision-making even if the interest might not comprise a conflict of interest.

"Thus, the fact that Ms Berejiklian disclosed interests arising from personal connections from time to time does not necessarily mean that a "conflict of interest" relevantly existed or was thought to exist.

"Further, even when a "conflict of interest" exists, a Minister is not necessarily excluded by the Code from making or participating in a decision or other action. Where a "conflict of interest" exists and can be managed, a Minister may be able to continue to act despite her or his conflict. For example, where a Premier has a "conflict of interest" in relation to a matter before Cabinet, her or his Cabinet can approve the Premier continuing to play a role in decision-making in relation to the matter. But only if the "conflict of interest" is disclosed.

"The Berejiklian Ministerial Code of Conduct is not a criminal statute. Nor is it a source of civil liability cognisable in the courts. Rather, it is a Code that prescribes "standards of ethical behaviour" and "internal governance practices" that Ms Berejiklian and her Ministers set for themselves."

Well, exactly. And as Chris Merritt points out, it is for the political process to manage. Labelling a breach of that Ministerial code in the Act as 'corrupt' has enabled ICAC to do wheelies for its own amusement. Bit like tearing wings off butterflies, perhaps ...(behaviour, by the way, that reflects badly on the character of the one doing the damage and ought not to be quoted as a fun thing to do).

The matters investigated:

MR ROBERTSON: (a) First, allegations that Ms Berejiklian engaged in partial conduct or conduct constituting or involving a breach of public trust in relation to certain projects in Wagga Wagga advanced by Mr Daryl Maguire;

(b) Secondly, an allegation that Ms Berejiklian refused to discharge her duty under the ICAC Act to notify this Commission of possible corrupt conduct; and (c) Thirdly, an allegation that Ms Berejiklian engaged in conduct that was liable to allow or encourage the occurrence of "corrupt conduct" by Mr Maguire.

Allegation 2(a) – Conduct in relation to certain projects advanced by Mr Maguire 45. This public inquiry will examine the first category of allegations concerning Ms Berejiklian with a particular focus on two case studies: (a) first, grant funding awarded to the Australian Clay Target Association Incorporated; and (b) secondly, grant funding promised and/or awarded to the Riverina Conservatorium of Music in Wagga Wagga.

"47. We expect the evidence to demonstrate that, over an extended period, Mr Maguire was a strong supporter of certain building projects advanced by the Australian Clay Target Association and the Riverina Conservatorium of Music and vociferously advocated for government support for those projects within Government, including to Ms Berejiklian directly.

48. We also expect the evidence to demonstrate that Ms Berejiklian made or participated in the making of decisions and took other steps that advanced the building projects advocated for by Mr Maguire without disclosing to anyone within Government that she was in a close personal

relationship with Mr Maguire at the time that she took those steps. It will be recalled that, during First Public Inquiry, both Ms Berejiklian and Mr Maguire gave evidence to the effect that they were in a close personal relationship with each other from at least 2015 if not earlier."

52. Importantly, that obligation of disclosure may arise even if the officeholder thinks that they are able to compartmentalise their public and private lives.

53. That is for a number of reasons including that, in a particular case, there may be a risk that an officeholder's personal concern for another may – whether consciously or subconsciously – influence or be seen to have the potential to influence the performance of the officeholder's public duties. That risk can be avoided or managed if the risk of conscious or subconscious influence is identified and managed.

54. The disclosure of potential conflicts is of particular importance, we submit, in relation to very senior public officials such as the Premier and Treasurer.

55. We expect the evidence to demonstrate that various public officials were influenced in the steps that they took in relation to the building projects to be considered in this public inquiry by what those public officials understood to be Ms Berejiklian's support for, or interest in, those projects. We also expect that there will be evidence to the effect that a number of public officials would have acted differently had they known about Ms Berejiklian's close personal relationship with Mr Maguire."

As Berejiklian pointed out to the Commission, some questions put to her demonstrated an ignorance of how government works, how policies are promoted to the Premier by various members and how decisions are made. That ignorance prompted a notable animus. If the notion that pork barrelling is corrupt political behaviour, could it be argued that all elections are pork barrelling seasons – and corrupt?

AUTHOR'S NOTE ON TRANSCRIPTS
After watching the proceedings in real time, these transcripts are reproduced from the ICAC records; they are formatted in accordance with standard practice, which often presents the questions and answers in continuous format, requiring the reader to recognise the different speakers, usually separated by dashes (---) and from the context.

MR ROBERTSON: Just have a look on the second thing attributed to you after the second dash. It says "I've got you now, got you the 170 million in five minutes." Do you see that there?---Yep, ah hmm. Now, having been refreshed with at least some of the context, the fact that a reference to the Wagga Wagga Base Hospital stage 3 was in the preceding budget papers before this conversation with Mr Maguire, are you able to assist as to what you were saying when you were telling Mr Maguire on 16 May, 2018, that you had got him $170 million in five minutes?---

I can only make this assumption and that is that the money was already allocated in the budget but the issue is that members of parliament like to see it as a separate line item because it was a separate stage. He needs to explain to his community that that particular stage was being, was being funded. So the money was already there, it's how it's presented, and many colleagues often have those issues where a commitment is made or money is allocated and it's put up as a general line item, but they want to be able to explain to their communities that the allocation is actually there. So the money had already been agreed to by government, it had gone through the proper process, the relevant minister would have had to have made that recommendation, and my assumption would have been that it's how it was presented in the budget papers so that any member, including he, were able to explain to his community that the stage 3 funding had commenced.

And in fact I see from the budget paper there, the end date was 2022 and often the allocations are less in the first instance and then the balance of the sums are, are heavier in the, in the, towards the end of the project, when most of the capital works are undertaken. So I see from there absolutely nothing unusual. If anything, I may have, and I have no recollection of this, spoken to the Treasurer to make sure that it was presented in a way in the budget where the local member was able to confirm to the community that the commitment was being made. But as to the dollars, they were already in the budget. Nobody on this planet can get that amount of money overnight and I certainly would never have done that. I am a stickler for going through the processes, I am a stickler for making sure everything is done by the book and I would never have been able to pluck that money out of thin air over, in five minutes. That's just absurd, absolutely absurd.

MR ROBERTSON: So at least a possibility is that when you said to Mr Maguire that you had got him the $170 million in five minutes, what you in fact got him is not actual new money but a reference in the budget papers to money that had been committed in previous budget years. Is that right?---That could very well have been the case, yeah.

But do you at least agree that the intervention that you apparently engaged in on 16 May, 2018, getting $170 million in five minutes, perhaps simply getting it in the budget papers as opposed to getting new money, that's not the kind of intervention that you would have made for any other member of parliament?---That's incorrect. It would have been. I've had many instances where members of parliament are upset because we've made a commitment and sometimes in some portfolios a minister, or the line item might be planning money and in that planning money there may be several projects that are bundled up in that and members get anxious when they can't go back to their community and show the line item. So in subsequent years, and certainly when I was Treasurer, you often have a separate sheet of election commitments so that the general line items can be determined and demonstrated to the community. So, it, that's a question *of presentation and, and I would have absolutely done that for other colleagues, absolutely explained to them. In fact we even had supplements to the budget to satisfy colleagues' concerns that if a commitment had been made but money hadn't been spent yet, but the money had been allocated, that we made that transparent to the community. Of course I would have done that for other colleagues, in fact I have. And I'm very comfortable if you go and ask some of them ...*

MR ROBERTSON: So, what, you say at this point in time as Premier not as Treasurer, you would intervene to get the budget papers changed within five minutes or perhaps more accurately within about two hours for anyone who raised the kind of issue that Mr Maguire raised?---It's not so much having change, it's just to make sure that if, if a colleague is concerned about something, I would raise it with the relevant minister, whether it was the Treasurer or relevant minister. I mean, that is just par for the course. Certainly, members from time to time, they go the minister, they go to the Treasurer. I'm normally the last stop they come to. But, having said that, I would have treated any of my colleagues in the same way. And I understand as a member of parliament myself that if you have a commitment in your community, you want to make sure the community believes you, that the money is there. The money was there. It's a question of presentation. And any Treasurer would be cognisant of that. It's, often in the days leading up to the budget, there's a flurry of, of interventions and calls by members to make sure that what they've promised their community is, is evident there, so that is not unusual in the least. It's actually part of the normal process."

The Commission had been trying to catch Berejiklian in special treatment for Maguire; it failed. Maguire's suggestion that she get a second, private phone (to keep secrets, no doubt) was also batted away:

MR ROBERTSON: Do you have a recollection of Mr Maguire suggesting to you that you need to get a private phone?---Well, not until you've showed me this. But I never did.

Well, do you have any recollection of Mr Maguire making that suggestion by way of text or in some other fashion or is your only recollection what you can now see up on the screen?---This is my recollection. And that could very well have been for privacy reasons. I had no, I had no inclination to think that it was because he'd, he'd done anything wrong. It could have been for privacy reasons. But I was clearly not concerned because I didn't do any of those things.

But back to my question. Are you saying your only recollection of Mr Maguire saying anything to you about getting a private phone is the text message that we can see on the screen?---No.

You don't have an independent recollection over and above - - -?---He may have, he may have - - - - - - just let me finish my question - - -?---Sorry. - - - over and above what you can see on the screen at the moment?---Look, he may have well said it to me but other colleagues did, as well, because I was someone who didn't have a separate phone. I've always had the one phone. Many people, many of my colleagues have two phones, one private, one business. But because I was so busy and had, and was so stressed, I always kept one phone throughout my career. I never had two. Many people did and many people used to suggest that to me outside of Mr Maguire but I never chose to do that.

Would you at least agree, sitting there now reading that text, that it would be a matter of concern to you if Mr Maguire is raising a question as to whether or not you need a private phone?---No, not really. That's a privacy issue. It probably, many… it's not just he that suggested that to me. Many colleagues have also suggested that to me.

"He says, 'Yeah, got the bugbears on the rum.' Do you see that there? ---Yeah. Any idea what Mr Maguire might have been talking about with bugbears on the rum?---I have no idea what that turn of phrase --- It may well be an autocorrect issue.---I have no idea what that means."

I'll just go to the next intercepted SMS. See your response at the time. "Okay. Is everything okay?" Do you see that there?---Yeah. Now, having seen that message, would you like to reflect on your previous answer as to whether the reference to a private phone was something that raised some concern or issue for you?---I couldn't remember. But if I was worried, wouldn't I have got a private phone? If I was concerned, wouldn't I have taken action? I didn't.

Well, if you were concerned - - -

THE COMMISSIONER: But you were concerned, Ms Berejiklian, about something because you asked him if everything was okay - - -?---Yeah, I - - - - - - in the context of the conversation which had happened four days earlier concerning his summons to give evidence here.---Right. I can't remember what I thought at the time.

MR ROBERTSON: Well, can you identify any reason why the Commission wouldn't read the message that we can see on the screen as being an indication by you of some concern about the fact that Mr Maguire is suggesting that you need to get a private phone?---Well, only, only for, for the sake of privacy, I would assume, but I, I wouldn't have, if I was so concerned, why, I would have done it.

(Counsel assisting then seems to switch to vaudeville…) If we then go to the next intercepted communication. We'll do a few in a row. He says, "Yeah, got the bugbears on the rum." Do you see that there? ---Yeah. Any idea what Mr Maguire might have been talking about with bugbears on the rum?---I have no idea what that turn of phrase - - - It may well be an autocorrect issue.---I have no idea what that means.

And if we go to the next page, you'll see that on 9 July, you're not sure you knew what it means, either.---Right. So, yeah. Yeah. It says, "What, what does that mean?" Do you see that there?---Yeah. Yes I do.

He then responds and says, "Bugger"?---Right. If we then go to the next one. You then say, "Who's Bigger?"---Yeah.

(a pointless exchange … but a part of ICAC theatre perhaps)

***

THE COMMISSIONER: Didn't it strike you as curious, Ms Berejiklian, that after the long conversation on 5 July, when you had asked Mr Maguire and he had assured you on several occasions that he had done nothing wrong, that he then thought it a good idea to get a phone, which you say you at least thought could be for privacy reasons?---Mmm.

Did it not concern you that if he'd done nothing wrong, why did he now want to switch phones, presumably for some added protection that the phone he'd been speaking to you on 5 July did not afford - - -?---I think it would be normal human nature that you wouldn't want anybody to assume your private conversations were being listened to. I didn't, I wouldn't have taken it any more than privacy issues. If I was concerned about my privacy or I was concerned that there was any wrongdoing, I would have taken, had my own private phone, but I didn't feel the need to do that because I - - -

I'm asking about Mr Maguire, not yourself."

***

Coming more to the valid point of an ICAC probe, Mr Robertson eventually got round to the subject of Maguire's attempt to secure a commission on a deal that was relevant to public interest. How did Berejiklian react when she began to suspect something?

MR ROBERTSON: It was apparent to you that Mr Maguire had admitted that he was engaged in a money-making exercise for his own benefit, along with one of the people who were being investigated in the operation known as Operation Dasha?---Well, certainly on and around the days of 13 July I considered that possibility. I just didn't know. I was away. But certainly around the day, 13 July and the next few days, I was very concerned as to what might be occurring, I wasn't sure, and, and I was extremely concerned. But you were aware, weren't you, in short order of Mr Maguire giving his evidence on July, 2018, that he had admitted to being engaged in a money-making exercise along with Mr Hawatt, who was then a member of the Canterbury Council? That was the gist of Mr Maguire's evidence in that afternoon.---Yeah, I mean, I was aware of what was on the public record but nothing more than that.

You at least had come to the view by 13 July, 2018 that Mr Maguire had been lying to you in the past - - -?---Well, on that, on - - - - - - in relation to his association with property developers, for example? ---On that day, not before that day. On that day you were aware that Mr Maguire had been lying to you in the past concerning that matter, is that right?---Well, I had made that assumption but I, I wasn't definitely sure. I had made that assumption that something was awry, given the evidence that came out that day.

So you assumed that something was awry, is that right?---Awry, but I wasn't sure what it was, and I wasn't sure what had transpired. But I'd assumed that he hadn't been fulsome with me, but I wasn't sure at that time. Now, that subsequently changed but, so that day and the next few days, I was not sure as to what had transpired.

The thing that was awry, as you understood it, was that Mr Maguire may have been engaged in some kind of wrongful conduct.---Well, he was hanging out with people that were, absolutely. But I wasn't sure if that was the case. It was my concern that he had been caught up in others doing wrongdoing, and I wasn't sure about his involvement or the extent of it. But the fact that he was hanging around these people in itself, and the fact that he'd been caught up in this inquiry, at the very least put a cloud over him and his involvement.

It was at least clear to you, as at 13 July, 2018, that Mr Maguire had been lying to you in the past or had lied to you in the past in relation to certain matters that he had told you regarding things like relationships with property developers?---Well, potentially, yes, although I wasn't sure. I was just mortified that he was caught up in all of this because it was not, in my opinion at that time, not within his character. And I was shocked at what had transpired, and I had assumed he was caught up in something, but I wasn't sure as to the extent of it.

But from a public perspective, clearly there were questions to be answered. And so at least, is this right, at least your state of mind as at 13 July, 2018, after Mr Maguire gave his evidence, was that you were of the understanding that Mr Maguire had lied to you in the past regarding, for example, his relationship with property developers?---Well, I didn't rule that out. It wasn't a conclusion I came to but I had assumed he may have. He may not have been telling me everything but I wasn't sure. It was the, the shock of, the shock of what happened did question, did make me question everything. The shock of what I, what I was told and the shock of what I subsequently read definitely made me question things and I was, I was very confused as to what it meant and very confused as to what he had actually been caught up in.

It was at least an assumption or conclusion that you had reached as at 13 July, 2018, that Mr Maguire had lied to you in the past in relation to his relationships with property developers, is that right?---Well, I, I think I thought that on the day but then in subsequent days I wasn't really sure because it, the investigation was ongoing and he was professing his innocence every day, and I came to the conclusion that I, eventually came to the conclusion that I just didn't know but I kept racking my brain as to, firstly to what extent he'd been truthful and, and secondly to what extent the investigation was, was going to reveal anything further about his activities.

But, I'm sorry, you're agreeing or disagreeing with the proposition that as at 13 July, 2018, after Mr Maguire's evidence came to your notice, that you had concluded or at least assumed that Mr Maguire has lied to you in the past in relation to his relationships with property developers?---Well, on that day I definitely would have had that, that conclusion. That subsequently changed, but on that day I would assume that there was something untoward occurring because he'd been caught up in this cloud and, and I, I subsequently wasn't sure and subsequently I gave him the benefit of the doubt and the presumption of innocence. But on that day and the next few days I just didn't know, but I had made that assumption.

So are you saying that, what, on 13 July, 2018, you had reached a conclusion that Mr Maguire had lied to you in the past but that that conclusion somehow was adjusted or changed in further days?---Well, I just wasn't, I just, I was away, I hadn't been following proceedings and so I just didn't know, it was, I was over, absolutely overwhelmed with the shock and grief of what had transpired in the hearing because he had told me definitively that there was nothing to worry about, he had done nothing wrong, and yet that's not what transpired in terms of, of evidence, but I, I, I just didn't know. I was confused but on that day I knew that something was awry, I just didn't know what.

The evidence of 13 July, 2018 at least led you to question what Mr Maguire had been telling you, for example, on the long telephone call of 5 July, 2018?---Absolutely. I questioned everything. I questioned anything that I may have known, I questioned everything. That was, I can't imagine, I can't express what a shock it was to the system because you have a certain view of somebody and, and that view is then questioned, was enormously shocking and I did, I thought long and hard about everything. I thought long and hard for a number of days about what he'd said and what I, what, what he had said to me and, and, and what had occurred and, and that for me was a very, very difficult period and I was trying to rationalise what had occurred at the hearing, his protestations of presumption of innocence and, and, and what my responsibilities were.

You came to the view by the weekend immediately after his evidence that Mr Maguire had let down his constituents, the people of New South Wales and the New South Wales Liberal Party, correct?---I did. I, I put that in a statement. In the face of all of that, did you suspect that Mr Maguire may have been engaged in corrupt conduct?---I didn't.

Why not?---Because I, I assumed that anything he was caught up in was, was something that, on his part, was, was, was unintentional, that he wasn't aware of everything going on around him and I also assumed that this, the investigation of Dasha would come to a conclusion as to whether or not he'd engaged in corrupt conduct. But certainly in my experience, in, in what I have known of him, I, I didn't put it past him that he was caught up in something that perhaps he wasn't totally aware of, and that's probably the extent to which my concerns went. But I certainly didn't, never suspected him of being corrupt."

***

Counsel Assisting was keen – exceedingly so, employing a crude repetition technique – to establish that Berejiklian regarded Maguire as part of her family, because that word appears in the ICAC Act as a criterion for consideration in how a Minister must reveal such a relationship. The questioning was akin to an interrogation; the transcript gives only an approximation of how the excruciating exchange played on screen:

MR ROBERTSON: At least as at 12 April, 2018, you regarded Mr Maguire as part of your family?---I had very strong feelings for him but I did not, I wouldn't have regarded him as a relative.

As at 12 April, 2018, you regarded Mr Maguire as part of your family. Correct?---I had very strong feelings for him, yes.

So is the answer to my question yes?---No, I did not regard him as a member of my family. I had strong feelings for him.

So as at 12 April, 2018, you did not regard Mr Maguire as part of your family, is that what you're saying?---I would not have introduced him or, or, or regarded him as, as, as a member of my family.

So does that mean that as at 12 April, 2018 you did not regard Mr Maguire as part of your family? Is that your evidence?---I don't want to undermine, I don't want to diminish the strength of feeling I had for him, and I don't want to diminish that in any way. I had very strong feelings for him. But I didn't feel the relationship was at a stage where I would introduce him necessarily to my parents or my sisters or need to declare it, but I don't want to underscore what I felt. But I didn't always feel that was reciprocated and I didn't feel a level of commitment.

So what's the answer to my question, then? Did you or did you not regard Mr Maguire as part of your family as at 12 April, 2018?---I didn't regard him as a member of my family in the same way that I regard my parents or my sisters. I regarded him as a part of my love circle, part of people that I strongly cared for, but I, I wouldn't have put him in the same category as my parents or my sisters.

I'm sorry, I still don't understand what your answer is to my question. Did you regard him as or as not part of your family?---Not in a sense that there was a significant, a significant declaration to be made. I had strong feelings for him. I don't want to doubt, I don't want to underscore that.

Don't worry about declarations and things at the moment.---Right. I just want to know whether you regarded Mr Maguire as part of your family or not as at April of 2018?---In the same category that I'd regard my best friends, that I'd regard people who gave me emotional support, who made sure that I was taken care of. There were, if, if you're going to ask me that question, I would have also included my best friends and others in that category.

So does that mean the answer to my question is yes or no or something else?---Well, if I define, if you accept my explanation in terms of how I'd regard my other friends and how I'd regard other people in my life, yes, but not in a sense that I regarded it as, the relationship, as anything more significant than what I took it to be.

So Mr Maguire was of no different status to any of your other friends, is that what you're saying?---No, I'm not saying that at all. But I, what I am saying is in my mind he, whilst I expressed that from an emotional perspective and for someone from whom I derived emotional strength, I wouldn't have put him in the same category as my parents or my sisters. No doubt you have different relationships, as anyone does, with parents, siblings and things of that kind.

But I just want to be clear. I think what you're saying, but tell me if I've got it wrong - - -?---Yep. - - - is that at least as at April of 2018, you regarded Mr Maguire as part of your family, albeit Mr Maguire was of a different kind in that he had a – he was in a personal relationship with you as distinct from a familial relationship of a kind that a parent might have with a child, is that fair?---I'll accept that, yep.

Now, you saw in Mr Maguire's evidence he referred to the fact that he had a key to your, I think it's your current house, is that right?---He had, yes. He was given that key soon after you moved into your current house, is that right?---I can't recollect exactly the time.

> *"Do you agree that Mr Maguire, throughout the time of your close personal relationship with him, was a vociferous advocate for projects in Wagga Wagga?---Absolutely. He was extremely active, and I suspect he was as vigilant with many other colleagues as he was with me. But I also would like to state, Mr Robertson, so were a number of other colleagues."*

Or did he have key to your preceding house?---No, not that I'm - - - Did you ever ask for that key back?---No. I take it you've changed your locks since giving the key to Mr Maguire? ---I have. I have. I have.

You didn't change those locks, though, until last year, is that right? ---Correct.

You would accept, I take it, that a significant aspect of public trust in government is that public moneys be spent in the public interest? Do you agree with that proposition?---Absolutely. And can I stress, Mr Robertson, that every decision I've made has been in the interests of the public or the interests of the community or the interests of the government.

And does it follow from that that you would agree that probity in decision making regarding the use of public funds is important in the public interest?---I have lived my life by that. Every day that I have spent in public life I have done so, to the best of my ability, putting the public interest first, basing all of my decisions on what I regarded as in the interests of a community, of the state or the government, and I stand by that so strongly.

Do you agree that Mr Maguire, throughout the time of your close personal relationship with him, was a vociferous advocate for projects in Wagga Wagga?---Absolutely. He was extremely active, and I suspect he was as vigilant with many other colleagues as he was with me. But I also would like to state, Mr Robertson, so were a number of other colleagues. I don't think a day went by in public life - - -

THE COMMISSIONER: Ms Berejiklian ... Could I ask you to just answer Mr Robertson's questions and not make speeches.---Certainly, certainly.

MR ROBERTSON: Despite the answer that you were just starting to give there, I suppose you would accept, wouldn't you, that Mr Maguire, during the course of your close personal relationship with him, had greater access to you than what other backbenchers or parliamentary secretaries would have?---

I wouldn't agree with that. I think if you asked my colleagues, they would all feel that I was very accessible. When parliament was sitting, they would drop into my office and push their projects. They would ring me, they would text me. I would say that all of my colleagues had equal access to me, especially when they were pushing things in their electorate or if they were concerned about something in the community. So I would argue very strongly, and I would be very pleased for you to take a straw poll of all my colleagues, that I provided, I, I really prided myself on being a leader, on being a Treasurer, being a senior minister, that was accessible to all of my colleagues. All of them had my ear, to an extent.

THE COMMISSIONER: Ms Berejiklian, I don't think you are heeding the message I just communicated to you.---I appreciate that. Thank you.

"Are you seriously saying that Mr Maguire communicated with you as to projects in exactly the same way, that's your phrase not mine, exactly the same way as all of your other colleagues?---No. What I would say is that all of my colleagues had access to me in relation to advocating for their projects."

MR ROBERTSON: Even accepting or assuming what you've just said, you would have to agree, wouldn't you, that Mr Maguire had a greater level of access to you during the course of the close personal relationship than other colleagues, even though those other colleagues might have had a good level of access. Do you agree?---I wouldn't agree with that statement because I felt, and I still believe, that any colleague that wanted to raise anything with me or had a concern with me, whether through correspondence, through meeting with me, through talking to me, would have had access and, and I would be very pleased for, for, for that to be put to any of my colleagues, that I tried at all times, to the best of my ability, to the best of the time constraints I had, to be accessible to all of my colleagues.

I think you deny the proposition that Mr Maguire had more access to you than other backbenchers or parliamentary secretaries, is that right?---I, I would say that all of colleagues had equal access in relation to matters regarding their electorate. No doubt about that.

So does it follow from that that you deny the proposition that

Mr Maguire had more access to you than other backbenchers or parliamentary secretaries?---In, in terms of fighting for their electorates or fighting for their communities, I would regard that all of colleagues had equal access, including Mr Maguire. So does that mean you deny the proposition that Mr Maguire had more access to you than other backbenchers or parliamentary secretaries?---Yes.

Mr Maguire did in fact advocate to you directly in relation to projects that he was advancing, is that right?---But so would all my other colleagues.

So does that mean the answer to my question is yes?---The answer is yes, but so would all my colleagues. He didn't restrict his advocacy to you just through formal channels, such as written correspondence and communications with parliamentary liaison officers, is that right?---He advocated in exactly the same way that other colleagues would have. In exactly the same way?---Well, in terms of, if you mean by verbal, by, by discussing matters, I have colleagues drop in without notice pushing things in your electorate.

"So what personal benefit did you think that you might get as a result of any exercise of functions associated with your cousins?---Oh, well, I would have been concerned that they may be treated in a particular way or that they may, or, or it might be assumed that they're getting favour because they're related to me."

Are you seriously saying that Mr Maguire communicated with you as to projects in exactly the same way, that's your phrase not mine, exactly the same way as all of your other colleagues?---No. What I would say is that all of my colleagues had access to me in relation to advocating for their projects.

"Why didn't you declare your close personal relationship with Mr Maguire with a view to avoiding any perception of favouritism, to use your phrase, in relation to Mr Maguire?---We didn't share finances, we didn't live together. I was not confident in his level of commitment. I did not regard him as a member of my family and I did not regard there to be any impact on my public responsibility. And I did not think the relationship had a sufficient status for me to disclose it."

Well, are you saying that Mr Maguire advocated for his projects in exactly the same way as others?---I don't understand the question, but what I, what I am saying to you, Mr Robertson, is that every colleague has their own style and way of advocating, if that's what you're getting at, and certainly all of my colleagues would have felt they had access to me – I hope they did, I hope they felt that – in relation to advocating for their projects, and that could have been through formal correspondence, through dropping into my office, through calling me, through a number of different means.

But Mr Maguire's access was no greater or less than anyone else within members of parliament within your party, is that what you're saying? ---That's how I felt."

In a court of law, the above exchange would have been curtailed, no doubt, by counsel for Berijiklian objecting to the questioning on the grounds of counsel badgering the witness.

***

In the following telling exchange, Berijiklian tells the Commission how and why she declared family members. Mr Robertson, meanwhile displays a certain lack of understanding about such disclosures.

MR ROBERTSON: Ms Berejiklian, when you were a minister you understood that you had a duty under the NSW Ministerial Code of Conduct to disclose to the Cabinet or a Cabinet committee any conflict of interest and duty that arose in relation to any matter before Cabinet or a committee of Cabinet?---Yes. You were aware of that duty?---Yes, yes.

You were aware that you had a duty to ensure that any such disclosure was recorded in the official record of proceedings of the Cabinet or the committee of Cabinet?---Yes. A duty to abstain from participating in any discussion of any matter in respect of which you had a conflict of interest or from any decision-making in respect of it?---Yes.

And that you had a duty to not be present at the meeting of Cabinet or committee of Cabinet unless it was approved by the Premier of the day or the chair of the particular meeting concerned, is that right?---Yes.

As you understood it at the time that you were a minister, those duties extended to disclosing any substantial personal connection that you had in relation to a matter if that connection was one that could objectively had the potential to influence the performance of your public duty, is that right? ---My, my understanding was a conflict of interest related to some personal benefit, some private, personal benefit you might get, especially in relation commercial matters.

I see. So as you understood it, is this right, there would be no conflict of interest for the purposes of the NSW Ministerial Code unless there was a potential private benefit either to – potential private benefit to you as the minister, is that right?---A personal benefit, yes.

A personal benefit to you as the minister, is that right?---Yeah, yeah, yeah. So for example, building a hospital is not a personal benefit to me, it is a community asset. It is something the electorate needs. I would gain nothing but political favour or support from the community by supporting that project. So why then did you formally disclose under the Ministerial Code the fact that two of your cousins were employed in the New South Wales public service?---

Because they, they were family members of mine and they worked in departments where I may have been making decisions and they may have been involved in providing advice or otherwise.

So what personal benefit did you think that you might get as a result of any exercise of functions associated with your cousins?---Oh, well, I would have been concerned that they may be treated in a particular way or that they may, or, or it might be assumed that they're getting favour because they're related to me. So the reason that you at least made that disclosure was to avoid any suggestion that the cousins might get any favour by reference to any exercise of public functions by you, is that right?---Well, I just wanted to make sure that I fulfilled my obligations.

No, but back to my question. Do I understand your evidence correctly to be that the reason that you disclosed, under the Ministerial Code, that two of your cousins were employed in the NSW public service was to avoid any suggestion of there being any favour – that was your word – any favour to them in the exercise of your public functions?---I think it was a bit more than that. They were paid a salary to work in those agencies, they earnt their profit and keep. It was a direct financial interest and it was beyond, beyond that notion of favour. It was more about they earnt their living by working in those agencies for which, at certain times, I may have had authority or responsibility.

"But isn't that the sort of thing that when you're making decisions in relation to projects which Mr Maguire was a vociferous advocate for that would at least cross your mind?---But, Commissioner, those, respectfully, those projects were about the community, they weren't about a person ..."

So is this right? That was a disclosure because you saw that those individuals, what, could get a private benefit through the exercise of your functions. Is that what you're saying?---I just wanted to make clear that there was nothing untoward in relation to those matters. Nothing untoward including because you wished to avoid any suggestion that any decision-making function that you're involved in may have acted by way of a favour to those individuals. Is that right?---Well, it was more broader than that. I didn't want them to have any adverse impact because of anything that I did or said or acted upon. It might have been broader than what I just put but at least included what I put to you?---Yeah, it would have included that, yes. Is that the reason why you also made disclosures from time to time regarding people who you knew when those individuals were being put forward for potential things like committee appointments and the like? ---Yes, if I, if I knew them, if, if I felt, if I felt that there was an appointment made, to avoid any sense of favouritism or, or not so much that word, but to avoid any perception that everything was done aboveboard, I would have declared that.

Why didn't you declare your close personal relationship with Mr Maguire with a view to avoiding any perception of favouritism, to use your phrase, in relation to Mr Maguire?---We didn't share finances, we didn't live together. I was not confident in his level of commitment. I did not regard him as a member of my family and I did not regard there to be any impact on my public responsibility. And I did not think the relationship had a sufficient status for me to disclose it. And had I been in a position where I thought it was significant enough, I would have. But I didn't have confidence, I didn't have confidence that was the case and I didn't think it was significant enough for me to have to disclose.

I take it, you don't share finances with the cousins in respect of whom you made a declaration?---I'm, I'm a, they're, they're my blood, though. They're my family.

I take it that you don't share finances with those cousins. Is that right? ---No, I don't. You don't share finances in relation to the individuals who you knew who were put forward in relation to committees associated with the government?---That would be the case, yeah.

You don't live with the cousins or with those other individuals, I take it? ---No. I'm still trying to understand how you draw a distinction between making declarations in relation to people who you know. There was one declaration, for example, where you said, "I know this person because of attendance at functions," but not in respect of someone who, you confirmed this morning, you loved, you understood that he loved you, he had a key to your house and you had, for example, an emotional attachment. How do you draw the line between those two propositions?---Because for me, a, for me, a relationship which required declaration would have had more status in my mind. And I was very uncertain as to the status of that relationship. It was not, for me in my mind, it wasn't significant enough because I didn't know where it was going I didn't feel comfortable with his level of commitment. He would sometimes even be in Sydney and I wouldn't even know. I didn't feel that level of, that level of commitment or that level of status that would require me to disclose it."

This was a key issue for ICAC: they fought Berejiklian over the status of Maguire as 'family' in the meaning of the Act versus "family" in her own private meaning of the word. (See Counsel's opening statement) The Commission refused to accept a differentiation, because if it did, their case (such as it was) would have to be towed back to base. The following exchange coming on the afternoon of Friday, October 29, 2021 after a morning of the 'family' fight, demonstrates the desperation:

MR ROBERTSON: Ms Berejiklian, in relation to the Riverina Conservatorium of Music matter that we were discussing before lunch, you ultimately participated in decisions of the Expenditure Review Committee in relation to that matter, is that right?---Yes, that's my understanding. And you in fact participated and didn't declare any interested pertaining to Mr Maguire, is that right?---Correct. Why not?---Again, for the reasons I gave beforehand. This was a matter about the electorate, about the community. It was not a, a matter that would bring me any personal, financial or other benefit and it was simply a community matter.

Was a factor in deciding not to make any disclosure or declare any interest in relation to the RCM matter the fact that, as I think you said this morning, at least as you saw it, the relationship was not one of sufficient status?---Or in my mind sufficient status and insignificance, yes. But was that a factor exercising your mind as to whether or not to participate in the decisions concerning the Riverina Conservatorium?---Can you repeat the question, please?

I understood your evidence this morning, perhaps wrongly, that one of the factors that was relevant to your consideration as to whether or not to declare any interest concerning projects advanced by Mr Maguire, was that you did not consider your relationship with him to have sufficient status. Have I got that right?---Ah hmm. Was that a consideration that you took into account in deciding whether or not to make a declaration or disclosure in connection with the Riverina Conservatorium matter when it was before the Expenditure Review Committee?---Yeah, but the overwhelming consideration was that this was a matter relating to the electorate, to public office, to the community. It had nothing to do with what was happening in my private life.

So does that mean it was factor or not a factor?---About the significance of the relationship? Correct.---I, I don't think I would have taken that into account because it wasn't something that I thought I needed to declare. So it was at least a factor in relation to the ACTA proposal, is that right? ---No, no.

THE COMMISSIONER: So, Ms Berejiklian, do I get the impression from these answers you're giving to Mr Robertson in relation to whether or not you declared the relationship in relation to the decisions concerning the conservatorium that you did turn your mind to whether you should disclose it at the time?---I don't think I did, Commissioner, because - - - It never crossed your mind?---No. Because I didn't think it was something that I needed to disclose because it was something in my personal life and we didn't share anything in common apart from that close personal relationship. We led separate lives. I didn't feel it was at a state at which – the threshold for me was would I introduce him to my parents, would I introduce him to my sisters, was I confident it was going to be something to last a distance of time and I didn't feel that.

Well, that sounds like you undertook a fairly intense process of analysis of the issue, Ms Berejiklian.--- (The Commissioner seems to be elevating an everyday personal assessment to an 'intense process' for the purposes of the investigation.)

Well, I can, I would have – well, perhaps not at those specific times though. But isn't that the sort of thing that when you're making decisions in relation to projects which Mr Maguire was a vociferous advocate for that would at least cross your mind?---But, Commissioner, those, respectfully, those projects were about the community, they weren't about a person – because I would have similar feelings or biases with other colleagues for different reasons, you might want to persuade them to support you or you might want to their seat or, there's lots of interests that exist. But for me the threshold question was this is, for me, a question of how I conduct my public decision-making and it had, in my view, nothing to do with my personal life because it was on the merits of providing something positive for the community. It was, had nothing to do with what was happening in my personal life.

Just confining this issue to the period when the decisions about the Clay Target Association and the conservatorium was made, so 2016 to 2018. You were not in a relationship with any other person, as I understand your evidence, of the nature of that with which you were involved with Mr Maguire?---That's correct.

So none of your colleagues were in the same relationship with you as he was?---That's correct.

So there's no comparison, really, between what you do in relation to declaring a conflict of interest in relation to him as in relation to any other colleagues, wouldn't you agree?---Except, well, the benefit was only for the electorate, it wasn't for, for him and it wasn't for me. It was for the community and the public interest. It had nothing to do with what I might feel for him. It was actually a decision based on what is in the public interest and I think this is the key issue. In my mind, in my mind, there wasn't any, any conflict on my part because this was a proposal to be determined through the proper processes on its merits for the public interest. It was not for any other interest but for, does the community deserve this project, should the government fund this project and is it a decision that is going to benefit the community or the government. It was not a consideration of what was going in my personal life. And the very difficult thing is, Commissioner, if I can make this point, that many colleagues lobby us for many different things and you have a different level of affection or friendship or perhaps reasons for why you want to support a proposal and it's very difficult in public life to draw the, to make those, to draw that line. And for me the threshold question was did I think this was a relationship which was serious enough or of significant status to share with my family. I would not have wanted to expose anybody to them unless I was confident the other person felt the same or that it was something of that significant a nature. For example, if there was anything formal or anything that in my mind provided a level of commitment or level of any conjoinment or any – you know, our lives were very separate. As I said, he used to come to Sydney and not even tell me sometimes. So it wasn't, in my mind, whilst I may have had, and I did, I definitely did have aspirations, in my mind I was never sure if those aspirations would materialise.

MR ROBERTSON: But as at the time that you were making decisions concerning the Riverina Conservatorium project, or at least as at the time you were participating in ERC decisions, you regarded Mr Maguire as family. Correct?---Well, I've answered those questions and I don't have anything further to add.

THE COMMISSIONER: I think the answer to that is to answer Mr Robertson's question, Ms Berejiklian.---Not in, not in any legal sense but as someone - - -

MR ROBERTSON: I'm not asking about any legal sense. Let me do it this way. Can we go to the decision itself. Volume 31.1, page 27. I'll just remind you of the decision itself. This forms part, Commissioner, of Exhibit 466, the redacted version. So do you see there decisions concerning the 1 Simmons Street site?---Mmm.

You participated in those decisions. Correct?---Yes, if it was in ERC, ERC, definitely. Well, I'll show you this, then. Page 13 of volume 31.1, part of the same exhibit. Do you see there your name identified as attendee for the particular meeting?---Yes, I do. And I'll show you on page 24, the first page of the decision. Do you see there it was 12 April, 2018?---Mmm.

If we now go back, please, to Exhibit 521, so the telephone intercepts I showed you this morning, just keep that date in your mind, 12 April, 2018, Exhibit 521. And if we go, please, to the last page of that exhibit, last page of that exhibit, please. On the very same day, you're saying to Mr Maguire, "But you're my family." Do you see that there?---I do.

How can you possibly say that the relationship was not of sufficient status to consider making a disclosure with respect to it when on the very same day you're telling Mr Maguire that he's your family?---Well, that's a turn of phrase but it, I did not mean it in the context that I regarded him as family, especially not in relation to the code. The code is very clear - - -

So just pausing there. When you say, "You are my family," what, you didn't mean you are my family. Is that what you're saying?---Well, yeah. It was a turn of phrase but I certainly did not regard that as literal. It was my way of expressing what I felt at the time about him. It wasn't a, a definition that I, that I, that I was wedding myself to. It was a, it was simply a turn of phrase to convey to him what I felt, the close connection I felt to him. But I've often regarded other colleagues or friends as family or brothers and, in fact, I, I regard my closest friends as family. So, of course, this was a different, a different nature of feeling but I wouldn't take that one occasion, that one word as a demonstration of what I attributed to the status of the relationship.

THE COMMISSIONER: It was demonstrative of the deep emotional attachment you had to him, was it not, Ms Berejiklian?---Absolutely, but I had no assurance it was reciprocated or that it was going to lead anywhere, and that is the, the threshold question, with due respect, Commissioner, that I - - -

I think we'll decide the threshold questions, Ms Berejiklian.---Okay. I'm sorry. Yeah.

"... this was a black and white issue of a community issue and electorate issue. It had nothing to do with what I may or may not have felt about anybody."

MR ROBERTSON: Was one factor that you took into account in deciding whether or not you should make a disclosure the position that at least as you understood it, Mr Maguire didn't stand to obtain any benefit from the decision. Is that one of the answers that you gave or part of an answer you gave to the Commissioner a little while ago?---I, it did not cross my mind because for me, this was a black and white issue of a community issue and electorate issue. It had nothing to do with what I may or may not have felt about anybody. This had everything to do with was it a worthwhile project, was it of community benefit and was it something the government should support? It had nothing to do with my personal feelings. And I want to make very clear that in all of my decisions, I always separated what I felt personally or, or what I may have felt with somebody as opposed to what I did in public life. And I want to make that very clear. I, I worked my, I worked my guts out in the roles that I had. I always put the public interest first. I did not think there was any conflict because this was an issue about an electorate, about thousands of people who may have benefitted from a government decision, and on its merits, I made the decision on the merits of the proposal.

Could you answer my question, please?---Can you repeat the question? What I'm trying to understand is I thought you said in answer to one of the Commissioner's questions, and I may have this wrong, but a factor that was relevant to your consideration as to whether or not to make any disclosures to your colleagues within the Expenditure Review Committee was that, at least so far as you understood the position, the decision wouldn't confer any benefit on either you or Mr Maguire, is that right?---I can't, yeah, I can't say that I even considered disclosing. That would be too strong a statement. I don't think it crossed my mind at that occasion.

Well, what - - -?---It wouldn't have crossed my mind at that occasion to disclose it. What I'm trying to understand is the distinction that you sought to draw this morning between appointments – you remember I referred to, for example, the fact that you made a disclosure in respect to an appointment to a government board in relation to a person who you'd been to a couple of functions with respect to. You remember me asking you some questions regarding that?---Ah hmm. You remember that?---I, yes, I do.

I'm just trying to understand why you draw the distinction between appointments of that kind and decisions such as the decision I'm now referring you to in relation to the Riverina Conservatorium.---Well, appointment is a personal benefit to somebody because they gain status or whatever from that position. But this was a community project for the community. It was not something from which I would gain anything personally. And, frankly, the only benefit to the local member would be a rise in his popularity, which is what every single member of parliament seeks to do. The job of a member of parliament is to respond to community needs, to respond to what their community wants, to fight for those things, and to make sure they, they push every door to make that possible, and I didn't consider that I needed to make any disclosure at the time.

So is this right, in the case – at least as you see it – in the case of appointments, appointment to, for example, a government board that could confer a benefit on the individual, in which case you would make a disclosure as to whether you have a relationship in the sense that you've gone to functions with them or they're your cousin or something along those lines, is that what you're drawing attention to?---Well, I don't think they're, they're, they're not exactly comparable. But in terms of, I think we overcompensate in terms of the declarations we make as to whether or not we know somebody in the appointment context. But certainly it would be fair for me to say that I did not consider that I needed to disclose, at that time, any private or personal relationship, given that we were looking at matters pertaining to the electorate.

I'm not asking about that at the moment. I'm going back to the distinction that you were drawing this morning, where you said to me, in effect, don't worry about the fact that I made a disclosure in relation to the person I'd been to functions with before or my cousin, because that's something different, that's about appointments rather than the kinds of projects that you and I have been discussing during the course of today. Is that a fair summary of your evidence?---That's correct. And my – well, yeah, it's part, it's a part explanation in that this, for me, this was my public duty, making a decision in the interests of the community, making a decision in the interests of the government, and making sure that we had positive steps in regional New South Wales.

So is this right, at least as you see it, where there's some appointment to some office, which may or may not carry with it a particular fee, you would then want to make disclosures about they're my cousin, they're someone I've been to functions with, et cetera?---I wouldn't keep it that narrow. I think there is also an issue of circumstance and category, so I wouldn't, I wouldn't be so narrow in that definition. I would, I would say that at all times one needs to consider when one should do, or make those disclosures or those declarations, and in these instances, because there were community projects for the community, I didn't feel I needed to make any disclosure.

I'm not worried about the community projects at the moment. I'm trying to understand the distinction that you sought to draw this morning, which I don't presently understand, between projects and appointments. I think you're saying, tell me if I've got it wrong, that you – at least in your mind – took a different approach to appointments over projects. Do I have that right?---Well, for me the distinction is, is there a personal benefit where the person is going to get a benefit, which is not necessarily a community benefit. And that's, that's the issue.

And the possible benefit in the case of an appointment is that they may get the status of being - - -?---Or, or a fee. Or possibly a fee.---Or a fee or, or perhaps other opportunities. And it's also what is the normal course, I think it's fair to say my colleagues and I overcompensate as well to make sure that there is no perception in that instance of any bias.

So do I take it from that that you made some disclosures before appointing Mr Maguire as a parliamentary secretary, which of course is an office that carries with it an additional fee over a backbencher?---He was already appointed one. Premier Baird had appointed him. I didn't appoint him. I reappointed him. Yes, so when you reappointed him, did you make any disclosures? Because that was an appointment which might have a benefit in the way that you've just described.---Well, that was a position of public authority. No, I did not make any disclosures.

Well, I still don't understand then why is there no disclosure in relation to that appointment yet a disclosure in relation to someone that you've been to functions with from time to time?---Well, I did not regard the relationship as sufficiently significant, of sufficient status and, again, I separated what I, what I felt personally from executing my public duties. He was already appointed a parliamentary secretary by Premier Baird and he was always regarded as someone who carried much kudos in relation to rural and regional issues. So I would not have changed that position.

But Mr Baird presumably wasn't in any particular close personal relationship or otherwise with Mr Maguire.---No, but he would have been appointed to that position based on his merit."

While Counsel Assisting attempted to load up every question with a presumption of guilt, repetitiously, his questioning could be said to have inadvertently undermie ICAC's credibility.

Private, personal, intimate matters …

Perhaps the most reprehensible aspect of this investigation as it relates to Berijiklian, and the one that attracted the most criticism, was the treatment of private, deeply personal aspect of the relationship between her and Maguire. It is important to understand the full context of how and why that is a justified criticism.

On the morning of Thursday, October 28, 2021, Ms Callan, acting for Berejiklian, made an application to The Commissioner in the following terms, and Mr Robertson responded; readers may decide for themselves whether Ms Callan's or Mr Robertson's argument should have been accepted.

MS CALLAN: Commissioner, I have an application to make for orders under section 31(9) and 112 of the ICAC Act. I am advised by Counsel Assisting that in the examination of Mr Maguire and in his examination of my client, Ms Berejiklian, he intends to adduce evidence which raises personal privacy concerns of the highest order for my client. Mr Robertson tells me he intends to question both witnesses about details of their close personal relationship, seemingly to scrutinise the level of commitment or substance of that relationship. Commissioner, you have a discretion under section 31(9) to conduct a private session during this public hearing. It is a discretion you exercised several times last year when Counsel Assisting dealt with private, personal and intimate matters.

THE COMMISSIONER: On his application.

MS CALLAN: On his application, yes, I recognise that. On his application last year, Counsel Assisting indicated his position that the public interest favoured preserving the privacy of Ms Berejiklian and Mr Maguire in respect of such matters. As I understand it, this year his position has changed such that he considers there is a proper basis for exposing such intimate, private details in this public forum. In my submission, nothing which has emerged to date indicates any principled basis for that change of position, and my application today is made in the context of what has already been established in the evidence adduced last year. In my submission there is no public purpose served by plumbing the depths of the private life of my client about intimate details of this relationship, which she has already stated in evidence was a close personal relationship, which she did not assess was of sufficient substance for it to be made public.

"In my submission, the factors strongly favour adducing evidence in relation to private details of this relationship in private session, noting that doing so in public will inevitably lead to intense and irremediable publicity and public scrutiny, along with humiliation and harm."

Your Honour, ICAC's principle object is to expose and combat corruption. The Commission may, for the purpose of an investigation, be satisfied it's in the public interest to conduct a public hearing such as this one, but before doing so the Commission must consider the benefit of exposing to the public corrupt conduct and whether that public interest is outweighed by the public interest in preserving the privacy of the persons concerned. Even when ICAC decides, as it has done here, to conduct a public hearing, you, Commissioner, always enjoy a discretion to hold part of that hearing in private session if you consider that that is in the public interest. In my submission, the factors strongly favour adducing evidence in relation to private details of this relationship in private session, noting that doing so in public will inevitably lead to intense and irremediable publicity and public scrutiny, along with humiliation and harm.

THE COMMISSIONER: This may be difficult, Ms Callan, but are you prepared or able to define what you regard as the private details of the relationship?

MS CALLAN: Your Honour, I am hamstrung in the sense that I have a sense of what it is that Counsel Assisting is proposing to adduce by reference, for instance, to what occurred during the private examination. Making this application in public, it would defeat the purpose of the application for me to refer to those particular - - -

THE COMMISSIONER: No, that's why I asked you very tentatively.

MS CALLAN: - - - details but in my submission it would pertain to matters which some might regards as hallmarks or indications of the level of commitment or standing that that relationship enjoyed

THE COMMISSIONER: Yes. Yes, that's helpful, thank you, Ms Callan.

MS CALLAN: Yes. Your Honour, to the extent that Counsel Assisting - - -

THE COMMISSIONER: You should call me Commissioner, Ms Callan.

MS CALLAN: Sorry, Commissioner. Maybe I'll manage to keep track of that. To the extent that Counsel Assisting regards it as relevant and legitimate to use this Commission's investigative powers to scrutinise the details of the relationship, notwithstanding all that has already been explored in evidence on the topic, in my submission such evidence can and ought properly be dealt with by the Commission in private session, similar to the manner that occurred last year. And for these reasons, and those developed in my written outline of submissions of yesterday, as I said, I seek an order, or orders, under section 31(9) of the ICAC Act that the Commission hear evidence from Mr Maguire and Ms Berejiklian as to the details of their close personal relationship in private session. And I recognise, Your Honour, that such an order may need to be crafted with a greater level of specificity to define appropriately where the public interest and the balance lies, but accompanying such an order, I would seek a direction under section 112 for non-publication of such evidence adduced in private session. I should say, Commissioner, without in any way preempting your decision on this matter, if you are not persuaded to make such orders, I don't propose, as it were, to jump up and down in respect of individual questions. I recognise that to do so would be unnecessarily interruptive of Counsel Assisting's flow. I will be guided by Your Honour's decision and your reasons, to the extent they're expressed, as to whether and to what extent I seek to deal on an individual basis with any particular matter.

THE COMMISSIONER: Thank you, Ms Callan. Mr Harrowell, did you wish to say anything in relation to Ms Callan's submission?

MR HARROWELL (for Maguire): I will be very brief, Commissioner. Firstly, we support the application made by Ms Callan on behalf of her client. We also submit, as Ms Callan's done, that a private hearing is more appropriate and that it would also be appropriate to make an order under section 112 for all the reasons that my learned friend Ms Callan has set out admirably in her written submissions.

THE COMMISSIONER: Thank you, Mr Harrowell. Yes, Mr Robertson?

"... it would not be an appropriate exercise of this Commission's admitted discretion to hold part of a public inquiry in private by holding a significant portion of a public inquiry in private."

MR ROBERTSON: In our respectful submission, the applications that have been made should be refused, not by reason of any change of position on my part or on Counsel Assisting's part more generally, but by way of applying the same approach to the question of private details and privacy as was applied in the first public inquiry. I'll explain that in a little bit more detail in a moment. But can I start with dealing with the structure of the way in which we say you, Commissioner, should deal with the present application. In our respectful submission, the starting point is really section 31(8) of the Independent Commission Against Corruption Act. That subsection in very simple but emphatic terms says that, "A public inquiry is to be held in public." In light of that, in our respectful submission, generally speaking, it would not be an appropriate exercise of this Commission's admitted discretion to hold part of a public inquiry in private by holding a significant portion of a public inquiry in private. That would risk, depending on the circumstances of the particular case and accepting that no bright lines can necessarily be drawn in this area, that would create a risk of a public inquiry becoming a public inquiry in name only.

The particular discretion that you've been asked to exercise today is in the context of a series of decisions that have already been made by this Commission, and to which my learned friend Ms Callan drew some passing attention a moment ago. This Commission has already decided, pursuant to section 31(1) of the Independent Commission Against Corruption Act, that it is in the public interest to conduct a public inquiry for the purposes of this investigation. Before doing so, the Commission was required to, and of course did, have regard to the various factors in section 31(2) of the Act. They relevantly include "The benefit of exposing to the public, and making it aware, of corrupt conduct, the seriousness of the allegation or complaint being investigated, any risk of undue prejudice to a person's reputation" – I note the word or the adjective "undue" in that phrase – "including any prejudice that might arise from not holding a public inquiry." And, importantly for the purpose of the present application, "Whether the public interest in exposing the matter is outweighed by the public interest in preserving the privacy of the persons concerned."

So this public inquiry is being held in circumstances where the Commission has been bound to and has considered each of the four matters I've just drawn attention to, including importantly whether the public interest in exposing the matter is outweighed by the public interest in preserving the privacy of the persons concerned. Those factors help explain why there was at least some period of delay between the decision of this Commission to commence an investigation into allegations concerning Ms Berejiklian and any public statement in relation to that matter, in particular a decision to conduct a public inquiry.

What should be apparent, we hope, from what's occurred over the past week and a half or thereabouts is that the Commission has done very significant work in private over many months with a view to reaching a conclusion as to whether it is in the public interest to conduct a public inquiry. That decision having been made, that provides a framework in which the discretion under section 31(9) should be exercised. As Ms Callan correctly identified before, during the course of the first public inquiry, I made various submissions with a view to attempting to protect the privacy of Ms Berejiklian and Mr Maguire as much as could sensitively be achieved in the context of the allegations that were being investigated in the first public inquiry. As Ms Callan correctly observed, that led to on a number of occasions certain material being dealt with in private rather than in public. The analysis, in our respectful submission, is different in relation to this public inquiry having regard to the expanded scope of the allegations being considered in the public inquiry during the course of this week and last week. In the first public inquiry, it was sufficient to describe Ms Berejiklian and Mr Maguire's relationship as a close personal relationship without any further exploration in public in circumstances where the allegations were focused on Mr Maguire's conduct and to at least some extent on conduct connected with that conduct.

But in the present inquiry, Ms Berejiklian's conduct is of central relevance to this investigation, and associated with that is a core relevance to the nature and extent of Ms Berejiklian and Mr Maguire's relationship. In particular that is relevant to the question of whether Ms Berejiklian was relevantly in a position of conflict within the meaning of the NSW Ministerial Code of Conduct. On that topic, with great respect, it seems my learned friend Ms Callan's written submissions have proceeded on a misapprehension as to the relevant law and the correct construction of the Ministerial Code of Conduct. Can I have the Ministerial Code of Conduct up on the screen, please. It was attached to the opening statement that was made on Monday of last week. But it appears, with great respect to my learned friend, that there's been a misreading of the definition of conflict of interest in clause 7(3) of the Ministerial Code of Conduct.

That definition relevantly says, "A conflict of interest arises in " - - - (reading it) relation to a Minister if there is a conflict between the public duty and the private interest of the Minister." Now, pausing there, the phrase relevantly used there is "private interest", not "private benefit". Then, importantly, it says, "In which the Minister's private interest could objectively have the potential to influence the performance of their public duty." So that's the core definition. Is there a conflict between the public duty and the private interest in which the minister's private interest could objectively have the potential to influence the performance of their public duty. The use of the word "objectively" is an important one.

"I'm not suggesting for a moment that we or that the Commission should go into what I think my learned friend described as plumbing the depths of the detail of the relationship."

Ms Callan referred to evidence given by Ms Berejiklian in the first public inquiry to the effect that, according to her – that is to say, according to Ms Berejiklian – she didn't see the relationship of being of sufficient substance. That's not the test that the definition of conflict of interest invokes. It's an objective test. And to assess as to whether a particular interest is one in which the minister's private interest could objectively have the potential to influence the performance of their public duty, one needs to understand with some degree of detail – and I'm not suggesting for a moment that we or that the Commission should go into what I think my learned friend described as plumbing the depths of the detail of the relationship, that's not the suggestion at all. But the Commission needs to understand to at least some degree what my friend I think described as the hallmarks of the relationship, in order to assess that question of objectivity. To take an example. If in truth the nature of the relationship was along the lines of what Ms Cruickshank said in evidence this week she thought it was, a historical relationship that was not what Ms Cruickshank described as "a full-blown intense" one, then it is much less likely that any conflict of interest would exist than if, for example, the relationship was such that it was, to use Ms Cruickshank's phrase, "a full-blown intense" one.

The concept of private benefit, which seems to be the one underlying what Ms Callan says, in particular in paragraph 15 of her written submissions, is one that becomes invoked in a deeming provision that is allied to and appears in the next sentence after the sentence of the definition of conflict of interest that I read out a moment ago. That says, "Without limiting the above", which plainly enough is a reference to the definition of conflict of interest that I read out before, "a Minister is taken to have a conflict of interest in respect of a particular matter on which a decision may be made or other action taken if (a) any of the possible decisions or actions, including decision to take no action, could reasonably be expected to confer a private benefit on the Minister or family member of the Minister and the nature and extent of the interest is such that it could objectively have the potential to influence the Minister in relation to the decision or action." Importantly that sentence starts with the phrase "Without limiting the above", so clearly we say as a matter of construction one can't use the second sentence to read down or limit the preceding one.

And further, it's in the nature of a deeming provision, "is taken to have a conflict", such that if one as it were ticks the boxes in those sentences, then a conflict of interest is deemed to exist, but it doesn't follow from that – as our friends submit in paragraph 15 of the written submissions – that if you can't tick the box or the boxes, then no conflict of interest relevantly exists.

In our submission, in the way that we sought to explain in our opening statement, in particular paragraph 32 thereof, it's apparent from the way in which the NSW Ministerial Code of Conduct is drafted that, and I'll quote from paragraph 32 of my opening statement, "It is sometimes necessary for a Minister to disclose any substantial personal connection that she or he has to a person relevant to a proposed decision even if the Minister would not her or himself receive a private benefit if the decision is made."

So the opening statement at the very start of this public inquiry sought to make clear what at least Counsel Assisting regard as the correct construction of the Ministerial Code of Conduct in the relevant sense. If we're right about that, then that question of objectivity, by which I mean could a particular private interest, including a substantial personal connection, objectively have the potential to influence the performance of their public duty, if we're right, that question is an objective matter that this Commission has to consider as part of the consideration of the allegations that are the subject of this public inquiry.

In the face of that, in our submission the same kind of approach that we advanced in the first public inquiry is appropriate, namely, that the privacy of Ms Berejiklian and Mr Maguire should be sought to be protected as much as reasonably can be possible but without in such a way as to distract from or minimise this Commission's principal functions and the discharge of its duties in the context of a public inquiry.

As a matter of practice what that means, in our submission it is appropriate for you to permit me to ask at least some questions concerning what Ms Callan describes as "the hallmark of the relationship" because those matters are relevant to that objective consideration of the kind that I have identified. It's not to say I make clear that there should be something in the nature of what my friend described as "plumbing the depths of the relationship", but the Commission does need to inform itself, and it's appropriate in the context of a public inquiry that was only decided to be conducted after the Commission considered whether the public interest in exposing the matter is outweighed by the public interest in preserving the privacy of the persons concerned, for at least those matters of hallmarks of the relationship to be dealt with in public.

One other matter I'll just deal with in passing, and this is principally relevant to the position of Ms Berejiklian but not relevant to the position of Mr Maguire. Soon after Ms Berejiklian gave evidence in the last public inquiry, she made a number of public statements concerning the nature and extent of her relationship. There was an article, for example, that said something like "I was going to marry him but I won't speak to him again," something along those lines. There is a bundle of material which I tender in support of the submission that that I am now making, a bundle described as volume 36. The short point is that whilst, as I said in opening, generally speaking one is entitled to keep their private life private, the public duties ultimately come first and that may then cut away from that right in relation to privacy.

But secondly, in relation to Ms Berejiklian, she has of course chosen, and I don't say this critically at all, but she has chosen to say at least some things in public with respect to her relationship. In any ruling that you make, you wouldn't put any impediment at all in me exploring the nature of comments of that kind because Ms Berejiklian has chosen to make comments of that kind in public. That's a matter relevant though I say to Ms Berejiklian's position, not to Mr Maguire's position, and so it's a factor to be taken in to account but it's a relatively weak factor, we accept, because one matter that is properly considered and should be considered in deciding whether or not to accept or reject the application is the position of Mr Maguire, and at least so far as I'm aware, Mr Maguire has chosen to make no public comments regarding his personal relationship. So at least insofar as Mr Maguire's position is relevant, the last point that I have made in passing is not a weighty factor at all.

THE COMMISSIONER: Mr Robertson, have you considered adopting the approach which was taken in relation to some aspects of the evidence last year of actually hearing it first in a private inquiry and there then being a debate within that context as to whether or not all or some of it could be used in the public inquiry?

MR ROBERTSON: Yes, is the short point but I need to qualify that in at least two ways. First, in relation to what I might describe as the hallmarks, in my submission it's going to be necessary for me to deal with those 10 matters and it's appropriate that I be permitted to do that in public, in effect in a form of propositional form and so the kind of procedure that you've indicated, Commissioner, that was adopted in the first public inquiry is not suited for questions of that kind.

THE COMMISSIONER: Ultimate questions, in effect?

MR ROBERTSON: Ultimate questions, in effect, or at least close to ultimate questions, one level down, as it were. In relation to, for example, telephone intercepts, I apprehend that there may be circumstances in which the appropriate course will be to play those, or parts of them, in private first – as was done, for example, in the first public inquiry – then having any necessary debate as to whether they can and should be played in public and then that can be resolved. It'll depend on the particular case, of course.

You recall, Commissioner, there was an example where a telephone intercept was played in private. It wasn't repeated in public, but the core, in effect, propositions or indicia that came out of the telephone intercept were then dealt with in public. So procedures of that kind may well be appropriate. The second qualifier that I wanted to make clear though is that whilst we say the same kind of approach that was adopted in the first inquiry should be conducted in the second inquiry, the way in which that analysis arises in the second inquiry is different because of the nature of this public inquiry. In particular the allegations against Ms Berejiklian and the relevance of the Ministerial Code of Conduct, it was sufficient or at least largely sufficient in the discharge if this Commission's functions in relation to the first public inquiry to use the phrase close personal relationship without going into any particular details as to what that meant, because that was sufficient to deal with the allegations that were there being investigated against Mr Maguire. Applying the same approach to this public inquiry we submit will require at least some additional material becoming known in public that might not necessarily have been dealt with in public in the first public inquiry. Now, I appreciate I'm being a little bit cryptic in the way in which I put, as it were, the line between the two categories. It's not a matter, we say, that one can draw necessarily a completely bright line because it will depend in part on what evidence Ms Berejiklian gives. If she gives evidence that seems to be consistent with material that I have that I haven't dealt with either in public or private, it may be that that's simply the way in which that evidence can be left.

In the event that Ms Berejiklian gives evidence in respect of which it may be appropriate for there to be an explanation by reference to other material, then that might then make it necessary to invoke the kind of procedure that you indicated a moment ago, Commissioner, or it may be necessary to ask Ms Berejiklian or Mr Maguire for an explanation regarding that particular matter, perhaps in private in the first instance, and then hear any necessary debate in relation to whether or not that matter is deployed in public.

One other matter I should indicate as a matter of practice, practical and procedure, as I understand it, the public stream is the subject of a delay between it, as it were, coming out of my mouth and going out into the public. It's always open to either me or anyone else in the room to ask for the stream to be stopped for the purposes of making an application such as, for example, an application of the kind that Ms Callan has made today and/or an application under section 112 of the Independent Commission Against Corruption Act for a suppression order.

THE COMMISSIONER: Thank you. Ms Callan, did you wish to say anything in response?

MS CALLAN: Only this, Your Honour. In my submission, Mr Robertson has not advanced any cogent or persuasive reasons to proceed other than the approach that was taken at times in the first hearing and upon which you asked him a question, that is, in respect of evidence which is in the terrain, as he puts it, of assessing or addressing, my words, hallmarks or what may be perceived as hallmarks of a relationship.

That, in my submission, can and should be dealt with initially in private, and insofar as it is proposed that any aspects of that evidence ought be, as it were, ventilated or made clear in public session, that can be dealt with as it arises. In my submission, the strong public interest in preserving the privacy of these two individuals lend themselves strongly to such a mechanism, which would, if Your Honour's not with me as to the general approach, at least enable you to make considered decisions in circumstances where there is necessarily a level of uncertainty and fluidity as to what it is Counsel Assisting anticipates doing and, in fact, does by way of questions asked or matters raised, documentary or otherwise."

(SHORT ADJOURNMENT)

THE COMMISSIONER: I reject Ms Callan and Mr Harrowell's application that evidence as to the details of Mr Maguire and Ms Berejiklian's relationship be heard in private pursuant to section 31(9) of the Independent Commission Against Corruption Act. In my view it is not in the public interest that I make such an order. I will publish my reasons for refusing the application in due course.[1] *Yes, Mr Robertson.*

MR ROBERTSON: I call Daryl Maguire."

There followed a series of questions to Maguire regarding land deals at Badgery's Creek and related matters. Then Mr Robertson turned to the personal:

Now, I'm sorry to have to do this but I'm going to ask you some questions about the nature of your relationship with Ms Berejiklian - - -?---Yes. - - - pursuant to the ruling of that the Commissioner made a moment ago. I just want to start by reminding you of the evidence that you gave on that topic in the first public inquiry so I'm going to take you to Exhibit 372 on that topic, which is a document that's been publicly available since last year. Exhibit 372. We'll go first to page 1714. Exhibit 372, page 2 of that exhibit 40 which is page – sorry, page 1 of that exhibit which is page 1714 of the public transcript. If you just look above the black box. We'll just zoom in to the middle of the page, please. Just a little bit further down, please, just above the top of the box. Can you see there I say, "Would it be fair to say that you were in a close personal relationship with Ms Berejiklian in

1. The Commissioner's reasons were published in a 6-page, 33 paragraph document on November 1, 2021. The essence of her reasons are in pars 31 & 32:
31. As Mr Robertson submitted, to make a blanket order requiring the relationship evidence to be heard in private and make a s 112 order preventing it from being made public as Ms Callan sought, would be to make the public inquiry illusory. It would detract from the important role a public inquiry plays "in … disclosing the ICAC's investigative processes."
32. It is not possible accordingly, as Ms Callan effectively argued, to contend that the relationship evidence is peripheral to the allegations being investigated. That evidence is intrinsically bound up in, and intersects, each allegation the Commission is publicly investigating concerning Ms Berejiklian. The relationship evidence should be addressed in the same forum as the evidence the subject of the Cabinet Documents Ruling so that the public can see the tension, if any, between Ms Berejiklian's discharge of her public duties and her private interests.

calendar year 2014?" And you say, "Yes." "What about 2013?" And you say, "Yes." Do you see that there?---Yes, I see that.

But then I should draw your attention to some further questioning on that matter. If we go to the next page of the exhibit, which is page 1805. The next page of the exhibit, please. And if we can zoom in around line 40, which is a little bit further down on the page. Do you see an answer at about line 39 you said, "But we had a relationship in '14, but I would call it a very close personal relationship definitely developed into '15." Do you see that there?---Yes. And then there's some further questions going both ways from you and me.

"It was a relationship, I take it, that was attended by a level of physical intimacy? ---Later, yes, yes. That's correct."

But if we go to the next page just to close off that questioning. Do you see there, "At least from your perspective were you in a close personal relationship with Ms Berejiklian at some time in calendar year 2014?" Do you see that there?---Yes. The answer was, "At some time." And then I make clear, "That's obviously from your perspective." And you say, "Yes, yes." Do you see that there? ---Correct. You and I both used the phrase "close personal relationship" and I think you used the "very close personal relationship" from 2015.---Ah hmm.

And I think your evidence in the public inquiry was, at least so far as you were concerned, you remained in a close personal relationship until briefly before the last public inquiry last year. Is that right?---Yes.

It at least continued during the second half of calendar year 2018, from your perspective. Is that right?---That's correct. You and I both used the phrase "close personal relationship" or in your case "very close personal relationship". I take it that that included a close emotional attachment?--- Yes. We had our moments, but, yes.

You loved her?---Yes. So far as you as you could ascertain, she loved you as well?---Yes.

You would stay with her, from time to time, when you were in Sydney? ---Yes.

She would stay with you from time to time when she was in Wagga?--- Yes.

You holidayed together from time to time?---Yes. You had a key to her house?---Yes. Did she ever ask for that key back?---No.

You contemplated marriage - - -?---Yes. - - - with her?---Yes.

There was discussion about potentially having a child?---Yes.

It was a relationship, I take it, that was attended by a level of physical intimacy?---Later, yes, yes. That's correct.

No doubt the relationship, like any relationships, had its ups and downs. Is this right, at least so far as you're concerned, the close personal relationship with the features that I've just identified or the hallmarks that I've just identified - - -?---Yes. - - - that was a continuous relationship from and including 2015 up to and including 2018 at least so far as you were concerned. Correct?---Yeah, we had a couple of spats in, in between, but, yes.

No doubt you had spats but not spats so as to say, well, the relationship's off, as it were, we can go and see other people? Nothing in that nature? ---Never. No."

Mr Robertson then turned to other matters, like the Clay Target Association. But he still managed to misunderstand the process of government decision making despite earlier explanations by Berejiklian. Or was it, again, framing questions with a presumption of guilt? (Oh, that's right, that would not be appropriate as the ICAC is not a court of law.) He asked Maguire *"I take it that you didn't seek to compartmentalise the public and private in the way that I discussed this morning, you didn't seek to avoid directly lobbying Ms Berejiklian regarding electorate of Wagga Wagga issues? ---No, I, I, I lobbied everybody. Anyone that had a, a slightest attachment to whatever it was I was proposing, I lobbied them. Including Ms Berejiklian, is that right?---Of course, of course."* And on Mr Robertson went in the same vein… *"So you accept then, is this right, that at least some of the communications that you had with Ms Berejiklian in relation to projects that you were advancing were done with a view to having her intervene?---Well, to take an interest, to take an interest and to understand the, the, the, the mess that the government had got itself in trying to, you know, get projects up and running, tied up in, tied up in red tape and rubbish."*

***

Margaret Cunneen SC and I were putting the finishing touches to our co-authored book *The Boxing Butterfly – Margaret Cunneen SC, a Career of Conviction* as these public hearings unfolded. Not only does Cunneen live in what was Berejiklian's electorate of Willoughby, she had her own ICAC roller coaster ride in 2015, which saw ICAC reprimanded by the High Court and by its Inspector for exceeding its authority in wrongly pursuing her.

Cunneen, who regularly boxes for sporting fun and studies martial arts, had been the target of an ICAC investigation - Operation HALE, in which her home was raided, phones seized - that ended in a knock-out, with ICAC and then Commissioner Megan Latham herself flat out on the legal canvas.

She was moved to comment on how the ICAC was treating Berijiklian:

"There was something very reminiscent of the morally judgemental 50s about the prurient attention to the detail of Ms Berejiklian's relationship with Mr Maguire. There was no reason for this detail to have been ventilated in a public hearing. Private hearings of personal detail would have been sufficient for a view to be formed about the existence and extent of the relationship. Had that occurred, reasonable people would have agreed that privacy, as to the details, is entirely appropriate.

"It seems to me that Ms Berejiklian's treatment was extraordinarily disrespectful and cruel. There is something most ungallant about a decision to air such detail about any woman's private life. In the 50s this type of material was much more damaging to the reputation of a woman than a man. Whether or not the decision-maker was channelling those times, the decision to go Public, for that part of the evidence, was designed to hurt. And it was an excruciating "punishment" delivered well in advance of any adverse finding."

Cunneen's response was echoed in the *Daily Telegraph's* Editorial of December 11, 2021, under the headline:

> **1950s shaming backfires**
>
> *FORMER Crown prosecutor Margaret Cunneen is characteristically blunt in her assessment of the ICAC's treatment of former NSW premier Gladys Berejiklian.*
>
> *She stopped short of using the words "slut shamed" but that is what she meant. Still furious about the shoddy way in which she herself was treated, Ms Cunneen said the tedious questioning about the personal relationship between Ms Berejiklian and her former boyfriend MP Daryl Maguire had a whiff of the puritanical 1950s and should have been held in private.*
>
> *Ms Berejiklian opened the door on the inquiries when she spoke publicly about her personal feelings for Mr Maguire but the labouring nature of the ICAC's questioning caused the maximum amount of*

embarrassment, quite outside whatever formal findings may or may not be made against Ms Berejiklian.

But rather than tarnish her standing in the community, the intensely private line of inquiry appears to have had the opposite effect. To a large number of voters, Ms Berejiklian emerged from the hearings a sympathetic figure, a person taken advantage of by a dishonest opportunist. She is seen by many as a woman who did not personally gain from her relationship or from her dealings with Mr Maguire – except for maybe an obvious sense of humiliation for being associated with him at all.

Whether or not you fully accept Ms Cunneen's assessment, the whole affair does raise questions about the ICAC's modus operandi and its level of accountability that should be re-examined, regardless of the outcome of this case.

A few weeks after the Prime Minister's remarks and Paul Kelly's criticism of the ICAC, Stephen Charles QC and Anthony Whealy QC, former judges of the Victorian and NSW courts of appeal, came to the ICAC's defence. Writing in *The Australian* (December 14, 2021):

"First, should an outside body make findings on breaches of ministerial codes of conduct? Or should it be left to politicians and bureaucrats to decide?

Second, is the definition of corrupt conduct in the NSW ICAC legislation too broad or too subjective; for example, "breach of public trust"?

Third, is there any justification for describing ICAC, as Scott Morrison did recently, as "a kangaroo court"? (ICAC is not a court at all. It is a standing royal commission.)"

As to the first question, the suggestion that the decision relating to a breach of ministerial standards should be left in the hands of politicians or their political servants is alarming. Two recent examples demonstrate why:

- *The sports rorts scandal: A confidential report by the Department of Prime Minister and Cabinet secretary dismissed without adequate reasons the careful and detailed investigation of the Australian National Audit Office.*
- *The carpark rorts scandal: More bizarre was the reaction of ministers to the ANAO report into these grants. Ministers contemptuously dismissed the careful findings that more than $500m in public funds had been expended primarily for political gain.*

If correct, as they surely are, these two ANAO findings are glaring examples of serious breaches of ministerial standards. Are we surprised ministers disagree? The most unreliable judges in these cases are politicians and their political servants.

The second question requires a better understanding of the NSW legislation. Admittedly, the definition of corrupt conduct is wide.

However, behaviour that otherwise would fall under the broad heading is excluded from consideration unless it could constitute or involve a "criminal offence, a disciplinary offence, reasonable grounds for dismissal or a substantial breach of a code of conduct". This limiting provision restricts the investigatory reach of ICAC to serious and/or systemic corrupt behaviour. It eliminates the trivial and insubstantial.

The concept of maladministration has no part to play in the legislation. It is not mentioned in the definition of corrupt conduct.

The concept of breach of public trust in the legislation is neither selective nor subjective. It is a concrete concept, well established in civil and criminal law. It underlay the separate convictions of Eddie Obeid in 2016 and again this year.

The third question involves the usual, tired attack on ICAC as a kangaroo court. As we have pointed out, ICAC is a standing royal commission. It is not part of the criminal justice system at all. We have had royal commissions aplenty in recent years: into trade unions, banks, institutional sexual abuse, aged and disability. Do we call these kangaroo courts? They hold public hearings and make public findings, often critical of individuals and institutions. Ought we not give them due respect for the important work they do?

The "three premiers" argument mentioned by Kelly has been refuted time and time again.

"Gladys Berejiklian was not compelled to resign because she was under investigation. That was her choice."

Barry O'Farrell, who has openly praised ICAC, chose to resign not because he was under investigation but because of his political embarrassment as a witness who had forgotten that he had been given a bottle of wine. Gladys Berejiklian was not compelled to resign because she was under investigation. That was her choice and no doubt supported by those close to her in her party. It was a political decision. Nick Greiner's case, decided in 1992, surely by now is ancient history.

The final example is the Margaret Cunneen case. ICAC has never conducted a public hearing or made any findings against Cunneen. Whether she acted appropriately or not has never been decided. The High Court halted the investigation at an early stage because it took a narrow view of the reach of the ICAC legislation.

It is significant that NSW then reinstated the broader view of the legislation in relation to serious cases. The Baird government thought it necessary to do this after receiving a report from a distinguished panel comprising Murray Gleeson and Bruce McClintock. It did so, consistently with the report, to avoid exposing public officials to serious corrupt influence from outside sources.

The broader definition has been adopted in other jurisdictions. The Cunneen case does not demonstrate in any way that ICAC acts as a kangaroo court. (The ICAC Inspector David Levine found otherwise and said, describing it as a 'debacle' in his scathing report.)

Rather than repeating the inaccurate views of the usual anti-ICACers, the Prime Minister and others might heed NSW Premier Dominic Perrottet's Sky News interview last week. Asked whether he thought ICAC was a kangaroo court, Perrottet said: "No, I don't", and added: "ICAC does a very important job and it gets rid of corruption from public life … We've seen over many years in NSW incredibly important work undertaken by the ICAC … And not just in uncovering corruption but preventing it as well and providing that advice to government. So I think they play a very important role here in NSW."

This suggests Perrottet, as have other premiers before him, values the ICAC as an institution worthy of respect. Morrison's disrespectful attack puts him on a collision course with NSW and with the broader community on the issue of integrity in public life."

At the end of that article, one reader, Michael, commented: "I'll tell you what's 'harmful to the quest for integrity in public life': a standing royal commission that creates the circumstances in which politicians feel the need to resign before any finding is made against them. Charles and Whealy are being disingenuous when they say that it was not an ICAC investigation that forced O'Farrell and Berejiklian to resign but their own political discomfort. It was entirely the immediate political threat posed by an investigation that forced the resignations. Not the outcome. That speaks to the bluntness of the ICAC's powers and the damaging nature of its processes. Both need to be reformed. Scott Morrison is right to be wary of the NSW approach."

"Charles rang Cunneen to apologise personally."

Another, David, wrote:

"As experienced lawyers , these authors should know that they cannot -and do not-speak for the "broader community". And they scrupulously skirt around the issue-is the public hanging out to dry of targets appropriate? It is the unnecessary public shaming which has caused the loss of two NSW Liberal Premiers, not the findings of ICAC. It is the public shaming which attracts , inaccurate but well-intentioned descriptions like "Kangaroo Court". Margaret Cunneen's legitimate complaint is that she was publicly shamed in circumstances where the High Court ruled that ICAC had exceeded its powers. Where corruption is found, following an enquiry, by all means make it public. However, until a result has been reached, the enquiry should proceed without the publicity."

The Australian published an apology on December 15, 2021:

Anthony Whealy and Stephen Charles, in an article published on the opinion page on December 14, stated it "has never been decided" whether Margaret Cunneen had "acted appropriately or not" in relation to an allegation that ICAC sought to investigate. In fact on

July 24, 2015, the NSW Solicitor-General found there was no basis for any charge. This decision was amplified in the December 2015 report of then ICAC inspector David Levine, which found the allegation had "no support in reliable, credible or cogent" material. The Australian apologises to Margaret Cunneen for the error.

FOOTNOTE:
The photo shoot for the cover of Boxing Butterfly, my book on Margaret Cunneen, coincided with the discredited article ... By a coincidence that a publisher would not allow in a novel, the assistant to our cover photographer, Emma Phillips, turned out to be the daughter of Stephen Charles. We have to report that soon after, Charles rang Cunneen to apologise personally.

WHO 'DONE HER OVER'?

These public hearings took place before **THE HONOURABLE RUTH McCOLL AO SC,** who was appointed Assistant Commissioner on Operation Keppell.

(The Hon Peter Hall QC is Chief Commissioner; Ms Patricia McDonald SC, Mr Stephen Rushton SC were appointed part-time Commissioners, both for five year terms from 7 August 2017. McColl had previously served in a same role from 1998 to 2000.)

McColl (born 1950) was a judge of the Court of Appeal of the Supreme Court of NSW from 2003 to 27 January 2019. Ironically enough, she studied in Berejiklian's electorate, at Willoughby Girls' High School, and went on to graduate with a Bachelor of Arts and Bachelor of Laws from the University of Sydney.

In 1980, McColl was admitted to the NSW bar. She was appointed Senior Counsel in 1994. From 1981 until 2001 McColl was elected as a member of the Bar Council of the NSW Bar Association and from 1999-2001 she was President of the New South Wales Bar Association - the first woman to serve in that position. From 2001–02, McColl was President of the Australian Bar Association.

McColl has also served as Vice-President of Australian Women Lawyers (1996–99) and President of NSW Women Lawyers (1996-1997). She has been a part-time Commissioner of the New South Wales Law Reform Commission, President of the Public Interest Law Clearing House (1999-2002), and Counsel assisting the Coroner in relation to the inquest into the 1997 Thredbo landslide.

Or as Daily Mail Australia likes to put it:

"The feisty corruption commissioner demanding straight answers from

Gladys Berejiklian is a former Supreme Court judge who blazed a trail for women in law.

ICAC Assistant Commissioner Ruth McColl has repeatedly reprimanded the former NSW Premier during a hearing into her secret relationship with disgraced ex-MP Daryl Maguire.

On Friday Ms McColl slammed Ms Berejikilan for giving unclear and longwinded answers to questions, a habit she perfected in her daily Covid 19 press conferences.

'Could I ask you to answer the question and not make speeches,' Ms McColl said."

McColl also has fans at justiceconnect.org, where she is a Patron of Justice Connect. Why? Because:

"Ruth McColl has been a long-standing champion for justice. Throughout her career, she has demonstrated exceptional dedication to using the law to help others, especially women and young Indigenous people.

Before being appointed to the Court of Appeal of the Supreme Court of New South Wales, Ruth dedicated her career to numerous philanthropic causes. She was a Member of Public Education Council (2002 – 2005), on the Board of the New South Wales Cancer Council, and a Member of the New South Wales Rhodes Scholarship selection committee (Chair 2007-2010).

From 1999 to 2002, Ruth served as President of the Board of the New South Wales Public Interest Law Clearing House – the NSW forerunner of Justice Connect. To have her join Justice Connect as a patron in retirement is testament to her commitment to justice, and making the law work for good.

"Justice Connect is an organisation that stands for something that I believe in very strongly – that the law can be used to make people's lives better, and the community more connected and vibrant." said Ms McColl."

***

COUNSEL ASSISTING, SCOTT ROBERTSON was called to the bar on 25 April, 2009. His professional self-description states that "Despite having a focus on commercial, construction and public law matters, Mr Robertson accepts briefs in a wide range of jurisdictions and areas of law. He particularly enjoys appearing in jurisdictions in which he is not a regular and in matters raising difficult or novel points of law or equity."

Otherwise, he is "a commercial (including building and construction) barrister with an interest and practice in public law. He has degrees in economics, international studies and law including a Bachelor of Civil Law (a Masters' degree) from the University of Oxford."

Coincidentally, Robertson also appeared, with J.K. Kirk SC, on behalf of ICAC at the 2015 High Court appeal against the Supreme Court decision in favour of Margaret Cunneen SC– which ICAC lost *(see later, ICAC- a damaged history)* Chief Justice Robert French chastised the commission's legal team for failing to provide particular documents to the court to assist during the legal argument. "I don't think I've ever seen this kind of scrappy hand-up before," Chief Justice French said.

(In that same appeal, Arthur Moses SC - before he became Berejiklian's new boyfriend - appeared with D.F. Jackson QC, on behalf of Cunneen. They won).

IN THE BEGINNING …

The origins of this investigation are to be found in Operation Dasha, an investigation into allegations concerning the former Canterbury City Council, "including whether certain public officials dishonestly and/or partially exercised their official functions in relation to planning proposals and/or applications concerning properties in the Canterbury City Council local area.

During the course of Operation Dasha (2016), telephone calls were intercepted between Mr Maguire and a former Canterbury City councillor, Michael Hawatt. Over the course of a number of telephone calls in May and 10 June of 2016, Mr Maguire and Mr Hawatt discussed commissions they could make from brokering the sale of significant development sites owned by entities associated by Charbel Demian. The proposed buyers in those transactions was the developer Country Garden Australia Pty Ltd, whose interests Mr Maguire purported to be representing. After those telephone calls came to the Commission's notice, the Commission decided to conduct an investigation into whether Mr Maguire's conduct constituted corrupt conduct, and the Commission did that of its own initiative."

Telephone intercepts later also revealed the relationship between Maguire and Berejiklian, triggering the subsequent investigation, "whether, between 2012 and 2018, the Hon Gladys Berejiklian MP engaged in conduct that:

constituted or involved a breach of public trust by exercising public functions in circumstances where she was in a position of conflict between her public duties and her private interest as a person who was in a personal relationship with the then NSW Member of Parliament,

Mr Daryl Maguire, in connection with: grant funding promised and/or awarded to the Australian Clay Target Association Inc in 2016/2017; and grant funding promised and/or awarded to the Riverina Conservatorium of Music in Wagga Wagga in 2018; and/or

constituted or involved the partial exercise of any of her official functions, in connection with: grant funding promised and/or awarded to the Australian Clay Target Association Inc in 2016/2017; grant funding promised and/or awarded to the Riverina Conservatorium of Music in Wagga Wagga in 2018; and/or

constituted or involved the dishonest or partial exercise of any of her official functions and/or a breach of public trust by refusing to exercise her duty pursuant to section 11 of the *Independent Commission Against Corruption Act 1988* to report any matter that she suspected on reasonable grounds concerned or may concern corrupt conduct in relation to the conduct of Mr Daryl Maguire; and/or was liable to allow or encourage the occurrence of corrupt conduct by Mr Maguire."

DARYL MAGUIRE

Daryl Maguire was appointed Opposition Whip on 7 April, 2003, and following the state election in March of 2011, was appointed as Government Whip. On 24 February, 2014, Maguire was appointed parliamentary secretary by then Premier Barry O'Farrell, and continued as a parliamentary secretary across a number of portfolios in the O'Farrell-Berejiklian governments, up until his resignation from the parliamentary Liberal Party on 13 July, 2018.

Maguire was also the chairman of the New South Wales Parliament Asia Pacific Friendship Group from 21 June, 2011, until his resignation from parliament.

GLADYS BEREJIKLIAN

Gladys Berejiklian was first elected to the NSW Parliament as Member for Willoughby on 22 March 2003. She was elected Leader of the Parliamentary Liberal Party on 23 January 2017 and sworn in as the 45th Premier of New South Wales. Gladys had previously served as Treasurer and Minister for Industrial Relations in the Baird Government since April 2015.

Prior to that, she was appointed Minister for Transport following the election of the O'Farrell Government in March 2011 and served in that role for four years.

She is a Master of Commerce graduate from UNSW and prior to entering Parliament worked as a General Manager for one of Australia's largest financial institutions. Gladys has also completed studies in Government and Public Administration (B.A., Uni. Syd).

In June 2021, Berejiklian revealed a new romantic relationship – with the lawyer who acted as one of her legal team at the ICAC investigation, recently divorced Arthur Moses SC. He and his former wife Sylvia have a son, Nicholas. Often thought to be Jewish, Moses is in fact a Lebanese Christian and has been a Berejiklian friend for some 20 years.

He has appeared in numerous high profile corruption investigations, advised and appeared for the NSW Crime Commission and for the former NSW Police Minister in the ICAC inquiry into political donations.

Moses regularly appears for the Commissioner of the Australian Federal Police in proceeds of crime matters.

One of his most interesting cases (by his own reckoning) was Hollingsworth v The Commissioner of Police in which he appeared for the applicant. The case involved a former stripper/prostitute/undercover agent in an unfair dismissal case against the Police. The applicant had been dismissed from the NSW Police Academy for failing to disclose her past.

The reader will forgive a 'truth stranger than fiction' detour here to elaborate briefly on Kim Hollingsworth, out of sheer fascination for a character whose dismissal from the Police Academy is the least of it.

It took two gos for Kim to be accepted to the NSW Police Academy, but she made a good start when in 1995 she was accepted. But when students started to learn of her past, she was subject to harassment and requests for sexual favours. During a detectives course, she was recognised as a former prostitute by a police officer who wanted her to work in his western Sydney brothel. She lodged a complaint – which came to the attention of the Royal Commission into the NSW Police – investigating police corruption. (See, there is a relevance…)

In meetings with staff assisting the Commission she named a further 20 officers who frequented brothels and strip shows. Hollingsworth subsequently stated that the Royal Commission encouraged her to return to prostitution to collect information on police involvement in the vice industry. Her flat was fitted with hidden cameras and she wore a wire to entrap the corrupt police officer, who by then was skimming 10% of Hollingsworth's income from prostitution.

In 1997 Hollingsworth appealed her dismissal to the Industrial Relations Commission of NSW (IRC). Commissioner Connor ordered the Police Service to reinstate Hollingsworth to her former position as student police officer and to pay her $35,000 for lost income.

The Police Service in turn appealed this decision and, on 22 December 1997, the full bench of the IRC quashed her reinstatement, noting Hollingsworth's deception of the Police Service at the time of her recruitment. The Commission noted, however, "room for sympathy for Ms Hollingsworth and the position which she is in, particularly after her substantial co-operation with the Police Royal Commission".

A counter appeal by Hollingsworth was determined in her favour by the IRC on 21 May 1999. The Police Service was ordered to reinstate her to her former position as a student police officer and to recommence her training with the next intake after 21 May 1999, and that the amount of $35,000 be paid no later than 28 May 1999

By the time of Hollingsworth's reinstatement, initial police training had been transferred to Charles Sturt University where students were required to complete three sessions of the Diploma of Policing Practice prior to appointment as a probationary constable. Hollingsworth agreed to participate in that program. Despite attempting to study at the College on three occasions however, she was subjected to harassment and ridicule from other students and left the program.

In 2006, then aged 40, Hollingsworth launched a last-ditch effort to join the Police Force. She returned to court and sought to enforce the earlier orders to be employed as a student police officer. The court found that the position had since been abolished, and it had no power to vary the earlier decision.

Following the success of the first two series of Underbelly, the Nine Network and Screentime Australia produced a third series, Underbelly the Golden Mile, set in 1989 Kings Cross. Hollingsworth's character (played by Emma Booth), featured in the series. Executive producer Des Monaghan said "It's a remarkable role because Kim Hollingsworth is a remarkable woman. Her story is one we've been interested in for a long time." Hollingsworth is described as "one of the series' most compelling characters". Hollingsworth was a key adviser on the production.

But it didn't end well. In December 2017 Hollingsworth (a dedicated vegan) was convicted of multiple animal cruelty charges and given a suspended jail sentence and ordered to pay almost $140,000 in vet and boarding bills. This was in regard to 40 horses in her charge and the 10th time Hollingsworth had been charged with animal cruelty.

ICAC - A DAMAGED HISTORY

"No good deed shall go unpunished..." that may be a bit of world weary wisdom burnt into the mind of former NSW Premier Nick Greiner, whose good deed was the establishment of the ICAC, which came into being in March 1989. For that well intentioned, good deed, the ICAC was the instrument of his political demise ... through no fault of his own.

In his second reading speech, Greiner said of the bill: "Nothing is more destructive of democracy than a situation where the people lack confidence in those administrators and institutions that stand in a position of public trust." He couldn't have imagined that the ICAC itself was to become one of the institutions in which public trust was to dissipate.

The allegations levelled at Greiner in 1992 were that he misused his position as Liberal Party leader to secure independent MP Terry Metherell's resignation from state parliament to achieve political advantage. Greiner argued it wasn't corruption, it was 'politics'.

Greiner was eventually cleared of corruption.

In 2014, a second Liberal state premier, Barry O'Farrell resigned after what he described as a massive memory fail in relation to accepting a A$3000 bottle of wine from Nick Di Girolamo, the then-chief executive of the company at the centre of the ICAC investigation, Australia Water Holdings (AWH).

O'Farrell had previously contended in evidence before the ICAC that he did not remember receiving the wine. It is alleged that AWH lobbied O'Farrell to facilitate the rolling out of water infrastructure with AWH and state-owned Sydney Water Holdings.

But a hand written note found in a drawer contradicted his claim that he didn't receive it. Much was made of the fact that it was a bottle of

Grange shiraz valued at $3,000. Another false positive case of corruption.

In its findings, reported on August 3, 2017, the ICAC said it was satisfied "that there was no intention on Mr O'Farrell's part to mislead".

In fact, no adverse findings were handed down to any Liberal party members including AWH boss Nick Di Girolamo who gave O'Farrell the wine.

To its shame, the current ICAC website still refers to how "The ICAC investigated allegations that the NSW State Emergency Service (SES) Commissioner, Murray Kear, took detrimental action against Deputy Commissioner Tara McCarthy, including dismissal from her position on 14 May 2013, in reprisal for Ms McCarthy making allegations to Mr Kear that SES Deputy Commissioner Steven Pearce had engaged in corrupt conduct.

The ICAC also examined allegations that Mr Kear improperly showed favour to Mr Pearce by failing to appropriately investigate allegations made by Ms McCarthy that Mr Pearce had engaged in corruption. It was also alleged that in relation to the above allegations, Mr Kear made false statements or attempted to mislead an officer of the ICAC in their exercise of their functions under the Independent Commission Against Corruption Act 1988.

In its report on the investigation, made public on 28 May 2014, the Commission makes corrupt conduct findings against Mr Kear. The Commission is of the opinion that the advice of the director of public prosecution should be sought with respect to the prosecution of Mr Kear for an offence under the Public Interest Disclosures Act 1994 of taking detrimental action in reprisal for a person making a public interest disclosure."

Yet in 2016, Magistrate Greg Grogin cleared Kear. "I accept Mr Kear did not make the decision to terminate the services of Tara McCarthy lightly or quickly," Magistrate Grogin told the court.

"I find that there were many factors behind the dismissal of Ms

McCarthy by the defendant - the inability of Ms McCarthy to assimilate into, cooperate within and lead the SES was, I find, the primary and substantial reason for her dismissal by the defendant.

"I am satisfied that the defendant did not dismiss Ms McCarthy as a reprisal, substantial or otherwise, for her making public interest disclosures. I find there was no element of revenge, pay-back or retaliation against Ms McCarthy by the defendant."

Magistrate Grogin said he accepted that conflict between Mr Pearce and McCarthy "caused the defendant great concern" and that he sought advice, counsel and assistance from a number of people within the emergency services community whom he respected, before he dismissed her.

ABC News reported (March 16, 2016):

"Outside court Murray Kear said he was relieved.

"It's like being in a brawl for two years and on the last day being told you're a good bloke," Mr Kear said.

"It's been a terrible journey for my wife, my family and all of my friends. I'm amazed at the support I got, but what really disappoints me is that it got to this stage - that we had to come to court to prove something that I think was obvious to most people from the word go."

He urged NSW Premier Mike Baird to look into the actions of the ICAC because the commission's probe into him had "ruined his life".

Mr Kear said he will be seeking costs after spending around $150,000 fighting the charges levelled against him.

Mr Pearce also came to court to hear today's verdict.

"It's public vindication ... it's been a debacle of an investigation right from the outset," Mr Pearce said.

"It's something that's impacted not just Murray Kear's career, but my own, also our entire families – financially, psychologically and emotionally."

But there is no mention of his exoneration on the ICAC website. There's integrity for you. Is it deep seated malice or profound incompetence that it has not been updated & corrected since 2016?

It is hard to escape the conclusion that the ICAC culture finds it difficult to tell right from wrong. Worse still, its 2015 pursuit of Margaret Cunneen SC suggests the culture is itself corrupt.

The ICAC allegation was that Cunneen had perverted the course of justice by advising her son's then girlfriend Sophia Tilley to fake chest pains to avoid a breath test after a serious car crash in which Sophia had been the not at fault driver. Neither Cunneen nor her son was present at the crash and when the ambulance took Sophia to hospital, her blood test showed an alcohol reading of 0.00. The ICAC was attempting to snare all three in the accusation and raided all their homes. (Why?)

In fact, Cunneen was not speaking to Tilley in an intercepted phone call; she was speaking tongue-in-cheek to the smash repairer who she knew socially from the pub, on the tow truck operator's phone, some time after the crash as the wreck was about to be towed away. The tow truck operator's phone calls were coincidentally being covertly recorded by the Australian Crime Commission in relation to other matters, totally unrelated to the job at hand.

It turns out that the reason ACC passed the information in the intercepted call to the ICAC was that Margaret had told the smash repairer that the owner of the car was the DPP. They jumped to the conclusion that Margaret had let someone else drive a departmental vehicle. In fact it was under an arrangement whereby senior public servants can lease a car for their totally personal use as a salary sacrifice part of their income package, but the "owner" is still DPP. So it all started with a stupid misunderstanding, by both agencies.

The ICAC didn't interview anyone at the scene of the crash. The ICAC didn't seek any information about Sophia's blood alcohol level from the

Police, who had the nil alcohol report within an hour of the crash. The ICAC wasn't interested in Sophia's blood alcohol level, only in Cunneen's professional blood.

Cunneen immediately took ICAC to the Supreme Court which ruled it a knock out in her favour. Gluttons for punishment, Megan Latham's ICAC wasted no time in appealing to the High Court. And in May 2015, when the High Court found the ICAC had been exceeding its jurisdiction for decades, it was an even more resounding defeat for ICAC.

At one point in the legalistic argument that is de rigueur at the High Court, Justice Kiefel made the following brief but irrefutable point, seeing the case from Cunneen's legal perspective:

KIEFEL J: *There would be the defence – I did not do this in the exercise of my official functions, I did it in my personal capacity. Therefore, it is not corrupt conduct and you do not have jurisdiction to inquire into it.*

Of course, Justice Kiefel's comment did not take into account that Cunneen had been accused by the ICAC of an offence she didn't commit – at all.

Writing for The University of Melbourne's 'Opinion on High' (a blog about High Court decisions), Martin Clark (a PhD Candidate and Judge Dame Rosalyn Higgins Scholar at the London School of Economics and Political Science and Research Fellow at Melbourne Law School) wrote:

"After reviewing the text, structure and context of the ICAC Act (see [36]ff), the majority emphasised that the symmetry of the structure of s 8 meant that 'adversely affect' in s 8(2) means 'to adversely affect the exercise of an official function by a public official in such a way that the exercise constitutes or involves conduct of the kind identified in s 8(1)(b)–(d)', that is, dishonest or partial exercise of a public power, breach of public trust or the misuse of information or materials in the course of official functions ([44]–[45]), which go to defining improbity in public administration at which the ICAC Act is aimed ([46] and see following).

The majority stated that the probity reading was reinforced by the many possible offences under the efficacy meaning that would range far beyond corruption (see examples at [52]), and held that:

It is not likely that an Act which is avowedly directed to investigating, exposing and preventing corruption affecting public authorities – and for which the justification for the conferral of extraordinary powers on ICAC was said to be the difficulty of discovering and exposing corruption in the nature of a consensual crime of which there is no obvious victim willing to complain – should have the purpose or effect of extending the reach of ICAC to a broad array of crimes having nothing to do with corruption in public administration apart from such direct or indirect effect as they might conceivably have upon the efficaciousness of the honest and impartial exercise of official functions by public officials.

Cunneen's victory in the High Court left the ICAC seriously weakened in the eyes of the public. It was further damaged at year's end after Inspector Levine's investigation into Operation HALE, which delivered a scathing indictment of an operation that should never have been contemplated.

The following are excerpts from ICAC Inspector David Levine's December 2015 report:

MARGARET CUNNEEN

Office of the Inspector of the Independent Commission Against Corruption

Report Pursuant to Section 77A Independent Commission Against Corruption Act 1988 - Operation "Hale"

ICAC Re Margaret Cunneen SC & Ors.

Page 49

... material obtained by the ICAC from Ms Cunneen's phone going back to 2005 was used for the sole purpose of a reference to the DPP

for consideration of disciplinary matters unrelated to anything up to that time with which ICAC had concerned itself.

Page 50

What to my mind simply cannot be explained or justified is the provision to the DPP of the five discs of all material (although a great deal of that related to the perversion of the course of justice aspect) but especially of the disc usefully for the DPP labelled "Journalist Disclosures" for a period going back to 2005. I am reinforced in expressing my gravest reservations as to the fairness and propriety of this step when I note that the DPP (Lloyd Babb SC) has concerned himself with but six text messages from 2012 between Ms Cunneen and a journalist friend. I am also concerned of course, as I have said, about the difficulty of Mr Babb's position when those texts are relating to him and a case in which he was involved as counsel in the Court of Criminal Appeal (see The Gilham Case) and in which Ms Cunneen was the prosecutor at trial which took place in 2012. The referral, as is conceded by the Commissioner was not on a confidential basis and no recommendation was made as to what action should be taken by the DPP.

What I would regard as the stark unfairness of nine years of the private affairs of Ms Cunneen and those of her friends (whether journalists or not) being placed before the DPP to fish for what turns out to be apparently six minnows in circumstances where the ICAC itself was not interested enough to even contemplate an investigation, virtually beggars belief.

This aspect of the conduct of the ICAC I describe, and I believe any ordinary reasonable person would describe, as unreasonable, unjust and oppressive.

Page 62-63

The allegation finds no support in reliable, credible, or cogent material, let alone material elevated to constitute evidence, of any conduct on her part, let alone of her son or his girlfriend, warranting the intervention and intrusive exploration by one of the most powerful agencies of the State.

Operation "Hale" from my point of view as Inspector, should be seen and, justifiably, can be seen, as the low point in the history of an entity whose functions, properly exercised, constitute an essential safeguard to the integrity of the governance of this State.

The ICAC media release, Wednesday 27 May 2015
(included for reference to the Levine report)

Since the NSW Parliament passed the Independent Commission Against Corruption Amendment (Validation) Act 2015 earlier this month, the NSW Independent Commission Against Corruption (ICAC) has been considering its incomplete investigations to determine what, if any, action it should take with each outstanding matter.

The Commission has determined to provide the evidence it has obtained in Operation Hale to the NSW Director of Public Prosecutions (DPP) pursuant to clause 35(4) of Schedule 4 to the Independent Commission Against Corruption Act 1988 (the ICAC Act).

Clause 35($) provides that "the Commission is authorised (and is taken always to have been authorised) to exercise functions under this Act on or after 15 April 2015 to refer matters for investigation or other action to other persons or bodies, or to communicate or provide evidence given to the Commission to other persons or bodies, even if the matter arose or the evidence was given to the Commission before 15 April 2015 and its validity relies on the validation under subclause (1)".

The Commission conferred with the DPP on 19 May concerning the referral of the evidence in Operation Hale.

Today, the Commission has furnished that evidence to the DPP for consideration of whether charges of attempting to pervert the course of justice and giving false evidence to the Commission are available against Ms Cunneen, Stephen Wyllie and Sophia Tilley.

The Commission has decided to take this step for the following reasons.

The Commission undertook an investigation into the alleged conduct of Ms Cunneen, Mr Wyllie and Ms Tilley after it was provided with information by a Federal law enforcement agency that indicated the commission of an attempt to pervert the course of justice by Ms Cunneen, a NSW deputy senior crown prosecutor, following a motor vehicle accident on 31 May 2014. It was accepted by the courts which examined the allegation in the course of the litigation initiated by Ms Cunneen that the alleged conduct could constitute an attempt to pervert the course of justice.

Any attempt to Pervert the course of justice by senior counsel, whether in the course of that person's duties or otherwise, strikes at the heart of the administration of justice and "is apt to give rise to public disquiet about the integrity of the judicial system"; Einfeld v R [2010] NSWCCA 87, Basten JA at [81].

The decision to refer the evidence is being taken by the Commission after an assessment of the reliability of the material which is to hand.

The Commission is of the view that it is in the public interest that the resolution of the allegations against Ms Cunneen, Mr Wyllie and Ms Tilley ought not be further delayed. The Commission is unable to finalise its investigation in Operation Hale as a result of the decision of the High Court in ICAC v Cunneen & Ors [2015] HCA 14 and

Part 13 of Schedule 4 to the ICAC Act only allows the Commission to provide to other agencies evidence it has obtained on or before 15 April 2015. Moreover, the pending review of the ICAC Act will not be completed before 11 July 2015.

It is also in the interest of those persons and the administration of justice in NSW that the evidence obtained by the Commission is referred for appropriate action to the DPP. The Commission's referral to the DPP also allows for the appointment of an appropriately qualified independent person from outside NSW to undertake that task.

In addition to considering criminal offences, it may be necessary for the DPP to consider whether disciplinary proceedings should be taken against Ms Cunneen. Accordingly, the DPP is the most appropriate agency for the referral of the material.

The Commission does not intend to comment further at this stage.

ENDS

Page 64 *(Levine report)*

(5) As to Media Releases, it should by now be obvious that great care and discretion be exercised in the composition of the document, the consideration of the purpose of its release, and the potential of the effect of its release. The Media Release of the 27th of May 2015 (see above), in my opinion, as I have stated, was so disproportionate to the merits of the whole enterprise as to amount to an unwarranted indictment of the people involved, an abuse of an undoubted power to keep the public informed, as to warrant the most trenchant of criticism. It was especially in the absence of any adverse findings, particularly unreasonable, unjust and oppressive. Nothing like it must happen again.

The Hon. David Levine AO RFD QC

4 December 2015

***

It is to be hoped that "nothing like it" will happen again, although this latest investigation – in its treatment of Gladys Berejiklian (called 'despicable' by one barrister) - suggests that there is some permanent inbuilt defect in the ICAC's culture. It will not repair and reform itself.

Perhaps the NSW Government will at last rethink and reform the guidelines and powers of this organisation so that it is indeed a protector not a predator.

The closest the Berejiklian government got to any reform concerning the ICAC was not very close at all. The subject was whistleblower protection and it came up in question time on May 12, 2021; Jamie Parker MP (Balmain) asked (Hansard): *I direct my question to the Premier. In April 2018 the Government committed to the preparation of a bill to protect whistleblowers who disclose to the ICAC, following recommendations from the parliamentary committee on the ICAC. The Government promised to deliver that by December 2019. It has now been three years. When will this important bill be introduced?*

Ms GLADYS BEREJIKLIAN (Willoughby—Premier) (15:20): I thank the member for Balmain for his question. I reassure him of the Government's commitment to making sure that this legislation comes to the Parliament. As the member might know but other members may not, we are guided in relation to that bill by the steering committee. I do have a positive update to give the member for Balmain but I want to stress who is on that steering committee. The steering committee is headed by the NSW Ombudsman. Other members of the steering committee include the Chief Commissioner of the ICAC, the Chief Commissioner of the Law Enforcement Conduct Commission, the Auditor-General, the Commissioner of Police, the Information Commissioner, the Public Service Commissioner, the Secretary of the Department of Premier and Cabinet and the secretary in charge of the Office of Local Government. We are waiting for them to provide us with the final bill so that we can present it to the Parliament.

All of those people, everyone would agree, are eminently qualified to be able to give the Government advice. Obviously the issue is more complex than anyone had envisaged, otherwise the bill would have come to this Parliament sooner. But please know that the time it has taken to bring this to the Parliament is in no way an indication of the Government's lack of enthusiasm for it. We want to make sure that it is right and we are relying on those good people to give us the bill in its final form. I understand that the draft of the bill was circulated on 5 March this year. The draft was discussed by the steering committee and several agencies have made written submissions to it. I understand discussion on issues arising from those submissions is ongoing between the Office of Parliamentary Counsel and the Ombudsman's office. I also understand that further instructions on the content of the bill were received on 5 May and the new draft is very advanced. That is the latest update I have.

Our hopeful expectation—but again it depends on the steering committee's recommendation and advice to us—is that discussions will be concluded very soon and the Government will have a bill ready for introduction hopefully in September this year. We have left it to the experts to provide us with the detail because it is a very complex issue. We want to make sure that we protect whistleblowers and also make sure that at all stages we do not do anything unintentionally to their detriment and that we cover everything that is appropriate. As soon as the bill is ready—I understand that it is in its final stages—it will come to this place. In response to the member for Balmain, I have not seen the draft or the final bill, but I do hope that, given the eminent people who have put it together, there will be widespread support for it when it comes to the Parliament.

The subject of the Ministerial Code of Conduct, such a central issue in the ICAC investigation Gladys endured, also came up in question time earlier in the year.

(Hansard) Mr PAUL SCULLY (Wollongong) (14:56): My question is directed to the Premier. Given the privacy obligations of ministerial staff under the code of conduct, what steps has the Premier taken to ensure that all her Ministers and their staff have had the appropriate level of training in data protection?

Ms GLADYS BEREJIKLIAN (Willoughby—Premier) (14:56): I thank the member for Wollongong for his question and say that my expectation is every single staff member should know their obligations under the NSW Ministerial Code of Conduct or the code that relates to their activity. Every Minister, every Parliamentary Secretary and every member of Parliament should know their obligations under the code of conduct and I expect at all times those standards are kept. I appreciate the importance of this issue and I appreciate the Opposition's questions about these issues. But I would also hope that whether it is the acting interim leader or other members those opposite would also ask questions about other matters that impact the community and the people of New South Wales. As the Premier of this State I am yet to be asked a question this week on jobs, on the economy, on health or on education. The issues raised are important. They can be asked a few times but repetitiveness does not assist. It is incredibly important for the future of New South Wales to have a strong and vibrant Opposition.

***

But the storm warning came in question time on March 23; we can almost hear the uproar when reading the Speaker's calls for order from the floor:

Ms SOPHIE COTSIS (Canterbury) (14:45): My question is directed to the Premier. ICAC has recommended Daryl Maguire face criminal charges for lying under oath about his involvement with the property developer

Country Garden. Given he told the Premier about his dealings with Country Garden in a phone call five months before he took the stand, why did she not tell ICAC what she knew?

The SPEAKER: Order! I call the member for Wakehurst to order for the first time. I call the member for Canterbury to order for the first time. I call the member for Keira to order for the first time. I call the member for Baulkham Hills to order for the first time. I call the member for Bathurst to order for the first time. I call the member for Baulkham Hills to order for the second time. I call the member for Canterbury to order for the second time. I call the member for Bega to order for the first time.

Ms GLADYS BEREJIKLIAN (Willoughby—Premier) (14:46): The New South Wales Government welcomes the report. There are a number of recommendations we will consider in due course, and the relevant matters there will be considered by the DPP.

That wasn't the first time Daryl Maguire had come up in question time. There was the following terse exchange on November 12, 2020:

Ms YASMIN CATLEY (Swansea) (14:28:45): My question is directed to the Premier. Will the Premier confirm revelations in the Legislative Council today that the corrupt former MP Daryl Maguire had a key to her house from the time that she bought the property in 2016?

Ms GLADYS BEREJIKLIAN (Willoughby—Premier) (14:29:05): I regret that Opposition members have started rehashing questions they have already asked me. What is clear to me is that the Leader of the Opposition and One Nation are very strong political allies. It is true. It just goes to show that the Labor Party will do anything in order to pointscore. I have finished my answer.

Ms YASMIN CATLEY (Swansea) (14:29:50): I ask a supplementary question. I refer to the Premier's previous answer. Did Daryl Maguire use the key that he had to the Premier's house to collect his personal belongings, including toiletries, two months ago?

Ms GLADYS BEREJIKLIAN (Willoughby—Premier) (14:30:12): I refer you to my previous answer and those last week and the week before. Ask me some real questions for once!

By then, though, the Daryl Maguire hand grenade had been lobbed at Gladys in true parliamentary style, as the following Hansard report demonstrates:

Ms JODI McKAY (Strathfield) (14:21:00): My question is directed to the Premier.

The SPEAKER: The member for Baulkham Hills will remain silent.

Ms JODI McKAY: Given revelations today that Daryl Maguire had a key and access to the Premier's home for several years, including as recently as last month, why did she breach her own Ministerial Code of Conduct by failing to disclose this relationship?

Mr Mark Speakman: Point of order—

Ms GLADYS BEREJIKLIAN (Willoughby—Premier) (14:21:38): I am happy to answer the question.

The SPEAKER: Normally there would be a problem with that question. It is the practice of the House to be respectful of the sub judice rule and of suppression orders that ICAC has made in terms of restricting publication or otherwise referring to material pursuant to section 112 of the ICAC Act. Balanced against that would be questions of privilege of the House and the public interest, but I will not rule on it given that the Premier has indicated that she is happy to answer the question. I flag that there would be a potential issue if the Premier had not been happy to take the question.

Mr Brad Hazzard: It is the first time in my 30 years in this place that I have seen any grub actually run against the order of ICAC.

Ms GLADYS BEREJIKLIAN: It is okay, Minister Hazzard. I want to make the following point in relation to the question the Leader of the Opposition put to me today, and I say this: Today, and in the last little while, I have heard and read things which are practically factually incorrect, and I have chosen not to respond because there is a process in place and none of us want to be in contempt of the process. If we have faith in the process, as I do, let the integrity agency do its work. I was asked to be there as a witness and a witness only, and I say—

Mr Michael Daley: Well then why did you go on Kyle and Jackie O?

The SPEAKER: Order! I call the member for Maroubra to order for the first time.

Mr Michael Daley: If you cannot say anything, what about your gossip columns on the weekend?

The SPEAKER: I call the member for Maroubra to order for the second time.

Mr Michael Daley: We cannot say anything now, but it was okay on the weekend and last Friday?

The SPEAKER: I call the member for Maroubra to order for the third time. He will leave the House if he continues.

Ms GLADYS BEREJIKLIAN: As I said, I have read and heard things said, including today, which are just factually incorrect. I will say this: I respect the process. I have faith in that process. I ask everybody to have faith in that process of which I was a witness, and I say this to the people of this great State, as I have said since I spoke as a witness and that is: Every day that I have held this office has been for the people of this great State. At all times our Government has put the people first and that is no different, and if those opposite or those elsewhere want to make things up, that is on their head and on their conscience.

And considering how the electorate of Wagga Wagga was on the collective minds of Daryl Maguire and Gladys herself through him, the following exchange on October 17, 2018 is worth noting:

Dr JOE McGIRR (Wagga Wagga) (15:15): My question is directed to the Premier. When will the Government provide a time line for the delivery of the commitments made to the people at the recent Wagga Wagga byelection, including the Tumut Hospital, the intermodal freight hub, the Wagga Wagga Base Hospital car park, and the work on the Gobbagombalin and Marshall bridges?

Ms GLADYS BEREJIKLIAN (Willoughby—Premier) (15:16): I thank the member for Wagga Wagga for his question and note this is the first question he has asked me. As the good member would know, both during and after the Wagga Wagga by-election I commented ad nauseam that we would adhere to all of our election commitments. As the member for Wagga Wagga and his community would know, this is in stark contrast to what those opposite did in Wagga Wagga when they were in government. Stages 1 and 2 of Wagga Wagga Base Hospital were promised by four different Labor Premiers and five or so different Labor health Ministers but it never happened. It was not until we came to government that the infrastructure and services the community of Wagga Wagga needs started being delivered.

Wagga Wagga boasts, and rightly so, its status as the largest inland city in New South Wales. It is a critical part of the future of our State. The good people of Wagga Wagga know that it is only a LiberalNationals Government that will deliver those commitments on the ground. They have lived through Labor governments and they got nothing. In contrast, we have made a number of infrastructure improvements and it will continue. This Government keeps its word.

THE DELAY

Counsel assisting the NSW Independent Commission Against Corruption, Scott Robertson, was due to have released its recommendations for findings into whether Ms Berejiklian had breached the public trust or encouraged corrupt conduct during her secret relationship with disgraced Liberal MP Daryl Maguire by December 20,

2021. However, a week earlier, the corruption watchdog announced that Scott Robertson would be releasing his confidential recommendations to the relevant parties by February 15, 2022. Gladys Berejiklian was to respond by March 28. Then a further delay was announced .... And in May, the ICAC announced it would organise a forum to determine of pork barrelling could be corrupt. That Forum report was released on August 1, 2022. Some unkind critics of ICAC are suspicious that the delays in finalising the Maguire/Berejiklian report were due to the ICAC having been spooked by the many critical comments published about its behaviour in that investigation. Especially stinging were comments that questioned whether political pork barrelling was really a business of the corruption watch dog. After all, pork barrelling is part of every election, practiced by all candidates in some form or other.

So it was no surprise that the report managed to squeeze out a form of words to justify (in retrospect, a bit like ICAC's legitimacy was secured in retrospect by the Baird Government) the investigation and to provide cover for its findings – yet to be released.

"Pork barrelling could be corrupt," is the headline. The statement announcing the Report says:

The Commission released its Report on investigation into pork barrelling in NSW (Operation Jersey), today (August 1, 2022), in which it defines pork barrelling as "the allocation of public funds and resources to targeted electors for partisan political purposes". In the report, the Commission finds that while individual matters should always be assessed on a case-by-case basis, a minister, for example, may engage in corrupt conduct involving pork barrelling, within the meaning of section 8 of the Independent Commission Against Corruption Act 1988, if the minister:

- *influences a public servant to exercise decision-making powers vested in the public servant, or to fulfil an official function, such as providing an assessment of the merits of grants, in a dishonest or partial way*

- *applies downward pressure to influence a public servant to exercise decision-making powers vested in the public servant, or to fulfil an official function, such as providing an assessment of the merits of grants, in a manner which knowingly involves the public servant in a breach of public trust*
- *conducts a merit-based grants scheme in such a way as to dishonestly favour political and private advantage over merit, undermining public confidence in public administration, and benefiting political donors and/or family members*
- *deliberately exercises a power to approve grants in a manner that favours family members, party donors or party interests in electorates, contrary to the guidelines of a grant program which state that the grants are to be made on merit according to criteria*
- *exercises a power to make grants in favour of marginal electorates, when this is contrary to the purpose for which the power was given.*

The report notes that those who exercise public or official powers in a manner inconsistent with the public purpose for which the powers were conferred betray public trust and so misconduct themselves. The Commission also finds that pork barrelling could satisfy section 9 of the ICAC Act. It may do so, for example, by conduct amounting to a substantial breach of the Ministerial Code of Conduct, or the Members' Code of Conduct, or conduct constituting or involving the common law offence of misconduct in public office.

The Commission notes that in issuing this report, it intends to make it clear that ministers and their advisers "do not have an unfettered discretion to distribute public funds. The exercise of ministerial discretion is subject to the rule of law, which ensures that it must accord with public trust and accountability principles.

Altogether, the Commission makes 21 recommendations to help prevent or better regulate pork barrelling. These also include that:

- *the Government Sector Finance Act 2018 be amended to mirror section 71 of the Commonwealth Public Governance, Performance and Accountability Act 2013 by including obligations that a minister must not approve expenditure of money unless satisfied that the expenditure would be an efficient, effective, economical and ethical use of the money and that the expenditure represents value for money*
- *the grant funding framework, or equivalent requirements, apply to the local government sector. This should include situations where local councils are both grantees and grantors*
- *clause 6 of the Ministerial Code of Conduct be amended to read, "A Minister, in the exercise or performance of their official functions, must not act dishonestly, must act in the public interest, and must not act improperly for their private benefit or for the private benefit of any other person".*

Readers do not need this author to deconstruct these statements of the obvious, such as the last point, above. Ministers must be honest, eh? Who knew?

A NEW DAWN, A NEW DAY, A NEW LIFE

The universe can sometimes display a wry sense of humour. The day (December 10, 2021) that a chirpy Gladys Berejklian told Ben Fordham on 2GB Breakfast that she was not going to contest any parliamentary seat and would instead be "going in a different direction" to start a new life outside politics, the NSW government (which she would officially leave on December 30, 2021) was running a tourism promotion TV campaign. The underscore was a play on 'NEW' from the name of the State, in a gutsy arrangement of the rousing song, *Feeling Good*:

It's a new dawn
It's a new day
It's a new life
For me
And I'm feeling good

"I'm a very positive person …" she told Fordham. "I'm ready to start a new chapter of my life …" It could have been a moment from *Soundtrack to My Life by Gladys Berejiklian.*

Gladys had rung in at 08:11 to wish Ben well on his last day for the year and thank him and everyone who had shown her great support and kindness. The radio interview followed a couple of weeks of public jostling while Prime Minister Scott Morrison, former Prime Minister Tony Abbott and others, had been wooing Gladys to consider standing for the seat of Warringah, to dislodge (supposedley) Independent Zali Stegall. Others had raised the uncertainty around the still pending findings of the earlier ICAC investigation, citing the potential problems if it found Gladys corrupt (however marginally and however wrongly in the view of her supporters). It would not be a political advantage, with all her political adversaries feasting on the Daryl Maguire affair and its consequent effects. Never mind the discomfort that she and her new boyfriend, Arthur Moses, might have to endure on a personal level. (A couple of months later, Midnight Oil fan Moses dragged Gladys along to their concert at the Qudos Bank Arena.)

Half an hour earlier in the same 2GB program, Fordham spoke to Dominic Perrottet who succeeded Gladys as NSW Premier … and when prompted by Fordham about calls for reforms to ICAC, it was a guarded, politically bland Perrottet who agreed that many government agencies need to be regularly reviewed, "and the ICAC is no different". But he was careful to praise the ICAC for having done "a very good job over the course of its life…" It was political cover that does not withstand scrutiny, but what else was the Premier to say on breakfast radio? The agency's darkly patchy history might make the morning listeners splutter into their cereal.

Whatever fateful coincidence was arranged by the universe, the two calls on 2GB were certainly relevant to each other. Fordham probing Perrottet about ICAC reforms, followed by Gladys in her post ICAC, 'new dawn' mode, behaving like a punching bag that bounces right back.

The universe moved quickly. Just two months after that radio chat, by Friday, February 11, 2022, Gladys had officially said "Yes" to Optus. Optus CEO Kelly Bayer Rosmarin announced her appointment to the newly created role of managing director of enterprise, business and institutional. There was probably a meeting or two and a private conversation prior to the announcement…. We might infer that in fact Optus had snatched Gladys from the market place as soon as Gladys had become available.

"Gladys is a proven leader who demonstrated her renowned strength, leadership, discipline, and composure in successfully guiding Australia's largest state through one of the biggest challenges in its history while earning the support and gratitude of the community for her tireless contribution," Ms Bayer Rosmarin said in a statement.

"She also builds and fosters loyal and dedicated teams who really go above and beyond for her."

"I believe she will be a game-changer for Optus."

Notably, the appointment was made well before the ICAC released its report on the investigation into Daryl and Gladys.

Then, on April 10, the 2022 Federal election was called, for May 21. As the candidates lined up to seek votes, Gladys was back in politics – campaigning with her mate and close former colleague Andrew Constance for the seat of Gilmore. Constance posted a photo with the caption: 'Great to have a true friend of mine down to say thank you to for incredible leadership of our region ! Love Glad,' Constance served as the New South Wales Minister for Transport and Roads in the second Berejiklian ministry from April 2019 until October 2021. He announced his resignation from State Parliament two days after Gladys resigned.

But it was on Wednesday May 4, 2022 that Gladys made her first sort-of-official but diplomatically silent appearance (in deference to her employer, Optus) on the political stage, at a function to support North Sydney's so called 'embattled' member Trent Zimmerman, fighting to retain his seat. His support for Gladys from the podium was amplified by that of former PM John Howard, the highest profile guest at the event. As they mingled, Gladys was seen and heard responding to another guest with a remark that a question about the then pending ICAC report apparently prompted, when she replied cheerfully "no, not yet …it might be another year before we know…but I'm getting on with my life." Cue the song - *Feeling Good…*

***

On January 1, 2022, the day after Gladys Berejiklian left the NSW parliament, the premier's office and politics, The Modern Slavery Amendment Bill 2021 (NSW) came into force. That was two and a half years after Gladys moved the second reading of the bill, which had been introduced by Christian Democrat's Paul Green. On June 6, 2018, in the Legislative Assembly, Gladys stood to speak in support of the bill:

From Hansard:

"I have the absolute privilege of introducing the Modern Slavery Bill 2018, on behalf of the Hon. Paul Green, MLC, for consideration by this House. As members are aware, the bill was introduced into the Legislative Council on 8 March 2018 and was passed with amendments on 3 May 2018. I urge all members in this place and people in the community to read the Hon. Paul Green's speech in the other place if they have not already done so. I thank the honourable member for his tireless efforts both inside and outside the House. I also thank his colleagues and supporters throughout the State for the efforts they have made to help raise public awareness about this important issue. I appreciate the intensity of positive sentiment in support of the bill and I again thank the honourable member for his leadership.

It is not every day that members of this place or the other place put forward something that will have a positive impact for literally thousands of people, and I commend the member for all his activity in this regard. For the benefit of members who may not be aware of the context or history of this issue, I will provide some. In November 2016 the Hon. Paul Green won the support of the Legislative Council to establish the Select Committee on Human Trafficking in New South Wales. In October 2017 that Committee released its report outlining a number of recommendations aimed at combating human trafficking and modern slavery. Also in 2017 two inquiries into human trafficking and modern slavery were undertaken at the national level, so the work here also allowed the issues to be dealt with at a national level. The report from the inquiry into human trafficking, slavery and slavery-like practices by the Federal Joint Committee on Law Enforcement was published in July 2017. The final report from the inquiry into establishing a Modern Slavery Act in Australia by the Joint Standing Committee on Foreign Affairs, Defence and Trade was published in December 2017.

The honourable member's bill addresses some of the findings and recommendations from the New South Wales inquiry, including the establishment of an Anti-slavery Commissioner, as well as some of the recommendations of the Federal inquiries. The bill has been developed by a cross-party working group on modern slavery, and I thank all the members of that group. I also thank the Hon. Paul Green for being present in the Chamber today. It demonstrates his absolute commitment to this and to ensuring that our House deals with the matter as respectfully as his Chamber has dealt with it. I assure him that that will be done. I have had the honour and privilege of being with the member at community events where he has expressed his views. It is extremely obvious that it is because of his depth of feeling, intensity, good work and goodwill that things have reached this point.

Slavery and human trafficking are transnational crimes that prey on society's most vulnerable people. They have many faces—human trafficking, servitude, forced labour, debt bondage, organ trafficking, deceptive recruiting, child cybersex trafficking, forced marriage and childhood brides. There is an undeniable moral imperative to take action in relation to all forms of modern slavery. The report of the Legislative Council Committee on Human Trafficking in New South Wales notes that since 2004 there have been more than 750 human trafficking and trafficking-related referrals to Australian authorities—I think many members of the community would be surprised by how high that figure is—and that the overall numbers of trafficked people in Australia may be considerably higher than that. According to the Global Slavery Index of 2016, it is estimated that 45.8 million people worldwide and more than 4,000 people in Australia are victims of some form of slavery. It is unacceptable that human trafficking takes place in Australia today and, on the back of the great work done by the Hon. Paul Green and the working group, this Government is committed to taking action to combat modern slavery in New South Wales.

I will now address the provisions of the Modern Slavery Bill 2018. The bill provides for the appointment and functions of an Anti-slavery Commissioner and strengthens relevant criminal offences. The bill comprises five parts and six schedules. Part 1 of the bill deals with the objects of the legislation, the first and foremost of which is to combat modern slavery. It makes provision for the Act to apply "to the full extent of the extraterritorial legislative capacity of the Parliament". Part 2 provides for the appointment of an Anti-slavery Commissioner. The bill proposes that the commissioner's functions include advocating for, and promoting action to, combat modern slavery. A primary role for the commissioner will be to prepare a strategic plan to combat human trafficking and raise public awareness about modern slavery. The commissioner will be responsible for educating and informing New South Wales residents about the warning signs of modern slavery. The commissioner will assist and work cooperatively with relevant agencies. The commissioner's role does not include investigating or dealing directly with individual cases. Part 2 also deals with the commissioner's responsibility for preparing and publishing an annual report, which will be tabled in both Houses of Parliament.

In division 4 of part 2 the bill establishes the Modern Slavery Committee as a joint standing committee of this Parliament. Part 3 governs modern slavery supply chains and imposes requirements on certain commercial organisations to report identified risks of modern slavery. Clause 25 of the bill requires commercial organisations operating in New South Wales that *have a turnover of not less than $50 million to publish an annual modern slavery statement. The statement will include information about steps taken to ensure that goods and services are not a product of supply chains in which modern slavery is taking place. Failure to comply carries steep penalties.*

Clause 26, along with amendments to the Public Finance and Audit Act 1983 set out in schedule 6.6, deal with government agency supply chains. The bill ensures that the NSW Procurement Board has power to direct government agencies in relation to steps to be taken to ensure that goods and services procured by and for government agencies are not the product of modern slavery. The bill also provides that the Auditor-General may conduct audits to determine whether government agencies are complying with those procurement obligations. Clause 27 requires the commissioner to keep a publicly available electronic register that identifies organisations whose goods or services are, or may be, a product of supply chains in which modern slavery may be taking place. The register will also identify any government agency that is failing to comply with directions of the Procurement Board relating to modern slavery.

Clause 28 enables the commissioner to develop and to make publicly available codes of practice that can be used to remediate or to monitor identified risks of modern slavery. Clause 29 enables the commissioner to promote public awareness of, and give advice on, steps to be taken to remediate or to monitor risks of modern slavery in supply chains. Unfortunately, all of us have likely unintentionally been party to modern slavery in supply chains—for example, through the clothing we wear, the technology we use and the food we eat. All consumers need to be educated to actively look at what they are wearing, eating and using to ensure that supply chains are slave-proof. The commissioner will play a critical role in raising awareness in business, government and among the public about best practice measures that we can take to ensure that supply chains minimise the risks of involving modern slavery.

Part 4 of the bill enables a court that convicts a person of a modern slavery offence to make a modern slavery risk order. The orders will prohibit conduct specified in the order, and a breach of the order will constitute an offence. Part 5 of the bill deals with miscellaneous components of the bill, including the regulation-making power. Schedule 2 to the bill contains the machinery provisions governing the procedures of the Modern Slavery Committee. Schedule 3 to the bill lists the relevant offences that are modern slavery offences for the purposes of the bill, and which are a key component of the definition of the term "modern slavery" in the bill. Schedule 5 to the bill sets out amendments to the Crimes Act 1900 to strengthen existing offences related to modern slavery and to introduce a range of new offences.

Amendments to section 91G of the Crimes Act 1900 create an aggravated offence of using a child for the production of child abuse material, where certain factors are present, and sets out increased penalties for circumstances of aggravation, including imprisonment of up to 20 years. Schedule 6 to the bill sets out amendments to other New South Wales Acts and regulations. These include amendments to the annual reporting requirements of government agencies, to make provision for the Auditor-General to conduct modern slavery audits, and to enhance human rights due diligence in public procurement.

I now foreshadow that the Government will be moving amendments to the bill in this House to ensure a smooth transition to implementation. The Government amendments will address the following five issues: appointing the Anti-Slavery Commissioner under the Government Sector Employment Act 2013, and ensuring the commissioner is independent in relation to advisory and advocacy functions; giving the proposed Modern Slavery Parliamentary Committee a broad remit to inquire into and report on matters relating to modern slavery; ensuring that the supply chain reporting obligations in the bill do not overlap with any future Commonwealth regulation of modern slavery; imposing a requirement on government agencies to take reasonable steps to ensure that goods and services procured by and for the agency are not the product of modern slavery; and removing from the bill a requirement for a modern slavery course in the school curriculum. We believe this policy objective is better considered through non-legislative means. I encourage all stakeholders to contribute to the review of the school curriculum that is currently underway.

As I have already outlined, the bill imposes a requirement to prepare a modern slavery statement on commercial organisations with a total annual turnover of not less than $50 million. This may include some organisations that we would regard as small businesses because they have fewer than 20 employees. The Government has received advice from the Small Business Commissioner about the regulatory burden on small businesses arising out of this provision. During the implementation process for this bill I will ensure that small businesses are exempt from the requirement to prepare a modern slavery statement for the 18 months following commencement. The Government wants to deliver a workable solution to supply chain monitoring by both businesses and New South Wales Government agencies that harmonises with the Federal approach currently being developed and does not duplicate administrative burdens unnecessarily.

The amendments proposed to the bill follow extremely constructive and consultative discussion with the Hon. Paul Green. I thank him for the time he gave to this bill. It was late last night when we had our most recent discussion. I thank him for his support and understanding because we all want to ensure a smooth transition and for the intent of the bill to be reflected in our Government's ability to implement it as soon as we can, and that is my intention. I have discussed these amendments with the Hon. Paul Green and, without putting words in his mouth, I appreciate his support for them and his dealing with us on these amendments. We want to ensure that appropriate State-based mechanisms are in place to combat human trafficking and modern slavery while we contribute to the coordination of efforts across Australia. These amendments again demonstrate our full commitment to taking the most effective action to combat modern slavery in New South Wales and to ensure a smooth transition to implementation of these arrangements.

I thank the Hon. Paul Green again for his passion, dedication and leadership on this very important matter. I do not use those words lightly. His leadership will ensure the protection of many innocent victims, and that is the key impetus for this bill. Naturally, the Government will work through implementation issues with the Hon. Paul Green and all relevant stakeholders prior to commencement of the legislation, which I anticipate will pass both Houses of the Parliament. I again thank the Hon. Paul Green. I commend the bill to the House."

***

In her inaugural speech on May 6, 2003, Gladys had paid tribute to 'the good people of Willoughby', saying: "Many of my childhood memories are of attending Armenian Saturday school at Willoughby primary school, as well as being involved in other activities, such as the 2nd Willoughby Girl Guides and local sporting groups. This experience taught me to be proud of my cultural background but, more significantly, to value the importance of being a good Australian. This includes being proud of my surname. I thank the good people of Willoughby who voted for me, even though they could not pronounce it." At the end, take a note of who was in the gallery, as acknowledged by The Speaker…

Her speech in full (Hansard):

Ms BEREJIKLIAN (Willoughby) [7.58 p.m.] (Inaugural Speech): "Mr Speaker, I stand tonight in this Parliament knowing how important families and communities are in allowing individuals to grasp their potential and the opportunities our great nation almost uniquely offers its citizens. Increasing pressures on families, exponential rates of technological change and continuing global uncertainty have meant that more than ever before we turn to our local communities to offer and to receive support, to effect necessary change and to define and express the type of society we are.

Residents of the Willoughby electorate have every right to place high expectations on me as their newly elected member of Parliament. In this, my first speech, I wish to pledge to all my constituents that for as long as I have the honour and privilege to represent them in this place I will always put my local community first. I will strive at all times to remember the words of Edmund Burke, who said, on being elected the member for Bristol in 1774, that a representative should:

... live in the strictest union, the closest correspondence, and the most unreserved communication with his constituents. Their wishes ought to have great weight with him; their opinion high respect; their business unremitted attention.

I will dedicate the next four years and beyond to proving to my constituents that their trust in me is well placed, because for me, first and foremost, politics is about people. Willoughby is a richly diverse electorate, from the bustling central business district of Chatswood to the quieter suburbs along the foreshores of Middle Harbour. In Willoughby we have an extremely strong sense of community. We have prominent chambers of commerce, Rotary clubs, progress associations, Lions clubs, church communities, Neighbourhood Watch groups and sporting clubs. Informal street meetings and gatherings amongst neighbours are frequent.

In Willoughby we have a strong and proud tradition of revering and supporting our ex-service men and women. The Chatswood RSL Club, Willoughby Legion Club and Anzac Memorial Club in Cammeray remind us that so much of what we have today is due to the men and women who defended our nation's honour in times of war. For me, it was also of a great deal of personal interest to learn that the fifth member for Willoughby, Edward Larkin, who was sworn into this Chamber in 1913, died on the battlefield of Gallipoli in 1915, alongside thousands of other young Australians. The plaque behind me in this Chamber recognises his ultimate sacrifice.

In Willoughby we are passionate about our natural heritage and environment. When in 1788 Governor Phillip set out to explore Middle Harbour he found a very beautiful and rugged foreshore unsuitable for settlement. Due to the rough terrain much of that foreshore was not touched for over 100 years and fortunately for the most part it remains in the same pristine state today. Willoughby Falls at Flatrock Creek, the unique architecture and streetscape of Castlecrag—ably protected by the local Walter Burley Griffin Society—the famous bridge at Northbridge, 1920s California bungalows and Federation homes dispersed throughout Willoughby, Naremburn and Artarmon are but some of the other unique heritage and environmental features within the area.

In Willoughby we welcome cultural diversity. Locals of many backgrounds contribute in every facet of community life. According to the 2001 Census, 55 per cent of constituents in Willoughby have at least one parent who was born overseas and 32 per cent speak a language other than English at home. Despite these natural attributes and a great sense of community, regrettably many State government services are deficient in Willoughby. Our police in Chatswood, in the centre of Sydney's fourth-largest central business district, should not be forced to work from an old home and demountable buildings which comprise the current police station. It is not even deemed fit enough to be opened to the public on police open days. The Coalition committed $1.5 million to fund the shortfall between private sector development of the site and the total amount that is required. I urge the Government to match this commitment. I put on notice that I will be pursuing it vigorously on this issue until the new station is built.

The unique character of our local neighbourhoods in Willoughby is being threatened by this Government's heavy-handed approach to planning and development. The wishes of the local community and the character of our neighbourhoods need to be considered in the wake of inappropriate blanket policies such as State environmental planning policy [SEPP] 5 and SEPP 53. Chatswood train station is one of the busiest on the northern line, yet there is no access for the elderly or disabled from the platform up to the station. How much longer must we wait for this basic service?

If you travel around the Willoughby electorate during peak hour you will notice frustrated bus commuters who spend too long waiting in long queues, especially in Naremburn, Cammeray and North Cremorne. Other areas such as Castle Cove require new routes. I have also recently learned about the cancellation of services from Willoughby bus depot and will demand that the Government reinstate these services. Traffic congestion throughout the electorate is a serious problem. But what incentive is there to alleviate some of the stress through encouraging public transport usage when current services are so lacking? This situation cannot be allowed to continue.

I will be vigilant also to ensure that Willoughby receives its fair share of public education funding. Thanks to the efforts of my predecessor, Peter Collins, and the local community, Chatswood High School remains, notwithstanding the Government's earlier decision to close it. But there remain grave concerns regarding access to public education throughout the electorate, especially in relation to class sizes, special needs education and general resourcing issues. I intend to set a rigorous pace in communicating with my constituents, in working with the many local organisations, in being accessible and by being an effective voice in this place on their behalf. The recent election in Willoughby was hard fought and the result was close. I want to take this opportunity to place on the public record that I look forward to developing strong working relationships with both Willoughby and North Sydney councils. I thank the Willoughby councillors who are here this evening.

From a very young age I was imbued with a great appreciation of all the opportunities I had and how fortunate I was to be born and raised in a country like Australia. My parents each migrated to Australia in the 1960s, met in Sydney and were married in the Armenian Orthodox Church in Chatswood, in the heart of the Willoughby electorate, in 1969. Our family involvement in the activities of the local Australian-Armenian community cemented my growing interest in community life. Many of my childhood memories are of attending Armenian Saturday school at Willoughby primary school, as well as being involved in other activities, such as the 2nd Willoughby Girl Guides and local sporting groups. This experience taught me to be proud of my cultural background but, more significantly, to value the importance of being a good Australian. This includes being proud of my surname. I thank the good people of Willoughby who voted for me, even though they could not pronounce it.

I am deeply thankful for the support I have received from my friends in the Australian-Armenian community, many of whom are here tonight and many of whom I have known since childhood. I take this opportunity to salute the contribution they continue to make to New South Wales and Australia, just as I salute the contribution made by all the culturally diverse communities in Willoughby.

Whilst I did not realise it at the time, my upbringing and the values instilled in me were core Liberal values. In a society increasingly cynical about the political process and organised institutions, I believe it is more imperative than ever to have a constant point of reference, a core set of ideals and guiding principles to rely on, an anchor when one's mettle is tested and tough decisions need to be made. For me, that anchor has been, and always will be, the tenets of modern liberalism. For me, the essence of liberalism is having the opportunity to pursue and achieve your life goals, irrespective of your background, and then give something back to society by ensuring that this opportunity is created for others.

Liberalism ensures that government will always support those in need and allows individuals to live freely so long as they do not impinge on the freedom of others. I believe the challenge of modern liberalism and the challenge of governments all around the world can best be summed up by John Stuart Mill, whose following statement is as relevant today as it was two centuries ago. He said:

There is a limit to the legitimate interference of collective opinion with individual independence; and to find that limit, and maintain it against encroachment, is as indispensable to a good condition of human affairs, as protection against political despotism.

I stated at the outset my principal belief that politics is about people. I strongly believe that governments should strive to achieve the liberal principle of equality of opportunity as opposed to the Labor Party's ideological position of equality of outcome. Labor's position thwarts innovation, and engenders mediocrity and conformity. In the context of modern State government, a key component to equality of opportunity is a strong education system—both public and private. I deeply appreciate the opportunities I have enjoyed as a product of the New South Wales public education system. I will fight hard so that all schools in Willoughby have the necessary resources to educate our successive generations.

The people we represent in this Parliament will have access to equality of opportunity only if they are provided with adequate essential services such as education, health, public transport, safety and security. To provide these services we need fiscally responsible governments and sound economic management. A well managed economy means that adequate services are provided where they are needed. It is therefore frustrating today, in 2003, to see that Labor is failing to deliver better services and standards of living to the people of New South Wales. Whereas the Federal Government made the tough but necessary decision to address taxation reform by introducing the GST and allowing the abolition of several State taxes, the State Labor Party has tried to sweep the issue of taxation reform under the carpet. [Extension of time agreed to.]

Despite record State Government revenues and budget overspending, services in New South Wales are deficient. Furthermore, the Labor Government has failed to create a climate conducive to business growth. And the result? The average taxpayer is now left bearing the burden of funding this Government's inefficient economic management. It is high time that State taxation reform was firmly on the public agenda. When the Labor Party came to power in 1995 it stated that there would be no new taxes and no tax increases. Since that time, Labor has introduced the insurance protection tax, the owner occupied land tax, the parking space levy and now we even have to pay tax when we go fishing.

It has also increased land tax on investment properties and registration on motor vehicles, and payroll tax has increased by 58 per cent during Labor's eight years in power. Alongside these taxes, revenue has exceeded the budget estimates by more than $3.3 billion in the past two financial years alone. In fact, in the past eight financial years the Government has increased its revenue in real terms by more than 34 per cent. It is of great concern that against this backdrop of rising State Government revenue streams, increasing taxation and the successive budget spending overruns, the people of New South Wales have had an inadequate return on their hard earned tax dollar. Waiting lists continue to blow out, our transport infrastructure is at breaking point, our classes are too large, and the list goes on.

My constituents in Willoughby have every right to demand to know why Chatswood cannot have a new police station or why the elderly and disabled cannot have escalators at Chatswood railway station, or why residents have to pay land tax on the family home they have owned and lived in for 30-odd years. But again the question beckons: If these additional revenue sources are not fixing the many problems we have in the delivery of essential services, or if they are not being used to ease the tax burden on the people of New South Wales, where exactly is the money going? For the sake of the hard-working taxpayers in Willoughby and across the State the Government must urgently address these legitimate questions. Furthermore, the Labor Government can ignore genuine tax reform for only so long, particularly with respect to payroll tax and land tax.

Payroll tax is a disincentive to job creation and business growth, particularly for smaller and medium businesses. The New South Wales payroll tax rate of 6 per cent is uncompetitive with the rates in Victoria and Queensland. The Government should have worked harder to stay within budget and delivered a program for reduction of, at the very least, a full percentage point on the payroll tax rate. As for land tax. Land tax on the family home needs to be abolished and the burden of land tax on investment properties needs to be reduced. The land tax on investment properties is indirectly a tax on tens of thousands of renters because landlords are inevitably forced to pass the increases to their tenants. Such increases also affect small business operators. There also needs to be greater transparency in the land tax valuation process to address concerns about massive and inconsistent fluctuations.

Beneath the Government's spin about its record of economic management lurks a series of time bombs, highlighting the need for more comprehensive budget reporting standards. Honourable members should compare this situation to where New South Wales could be today. We have the people, we have the resources, but we lack a State Government which can make the necessary tough decisions and which can manage the economy efficiently. Working in the financial services sector for the past five years has given me an insight into the many pressures placed on business. I thank the senior management of the Commonwealth Bank for taking a risk in entrusting me as the general manager for a core part of the bank's retail business, with business responsibility for over 2½ million customers

Australia-wide. I leave behind many friends and dedicated colleagues.

In politics it is almost impossible to achieve anything on your own. I would like to thank my friends in the Liberal Party, many of whom are here tonight, who through their loyalty, honesty and counsel have assisted in my development over the past decade. In this category I place my predecessor, the Hon. Peter Collins, QC, who served the people of Willoughby with great distinction for 22 years. His contribution to the good governance of this State has been outstanding, particularly in relation to the arts, health, Treasury and his leadership of the Liberal Party. I extend a special thanks to the two Federal members covering my electorate—Joe Hockey and Brendan Nelson for their mentorship and continuing support.

I would not be here were it not for the training I received in the New South Wales Young Liberals movement, and I will forever be proud of having served as the President of the New South Wales Young Liberals in 1996. The Young Liberals play a major role in the leadership of our country, and it is a testament to the organisation that both our Prime Minister, the Hon. John Howard, and State Leader, John Brogden, are former New South Wales Young Liberal presidents. I thank the Liberal Party Women's Council for assisting me to take my seat in Parliament—without quotas I might add—and for preparing me for what lies ahead. A special thanks to my friends on the State Executive, especially Sam Witheridge, to the staff at the State Secretariat, the party membership at large, and to my personal staff for their unstinting support.

To all the members of my campaign team, led brilliantly by Deborah Klika, and to all the members of my local conference, under the exceptional leadership of Peter Davidson, you were all with me every step of the way, including those long 13 days after the election. In the first instance you bestowed upon me the great honour of being your candidate and then worked tirelessly to ensure that I became the member. I regard you all as part of my extended family and am excited by what we can achieve together for our local community in the years ahead. It is special to have former Premier Nick Greiner here this evening. I thank him for continuing to inspire a new generation of Liberals. I also note the presence in the gallery of two former members of this Parliament and distinguished Ministers in Robert Webster and Wendy Machin, who I am proud to call my constituents and who have been of enormous support. As you see, the Coalition is alive and well in Willoughby!

To my father Krikor and mother Arsha—whose birthday it is today—thank you for making me believe, ever since I can remember, that the sky is the limit. A special thanks to my sisters, Rita and Mary, who have always been my strongest supporters. Thank you also to my uncle, Father Razmig, who continues to be a constant source of inspiration. I stated at the outset my core belief that politics is about people. At the end of my parliamentary career I would like to look back and believe that I have contributed to improving the opportunities and standard of living of the people of Willoughby and the people of New South Wales.

I am particularly moved by the words of Johann von Goethe (1749-1832), who said, "Treat people as if they were what they ought to be, and you will help them to become what they are capable of being." I am proud and humbled to be here tonight to represent the values of my family, my party and my community of Willoughby. These are things that will always guide my words and actions in this place. Thank you for your courtesy.

Mr SPEAKER: I extend to the honourable member for Willoughby my congratulations on her inaugural speech. I note the presence in the gallery not only of a large contingent of her family, friends and constituents but also the former Premier, the Hon. Nick Greiner; the Federal Minister for Small Business and Tourism, Joe Hockey; former Ministers Robert Webster and Wendy Machin; and the former member for Ryde, Michael Photios."

***

The 26 square kilometre electorate of Willoughby covers parts* or all of the suburbs of Artarmon*, Cammeray, Castlecrag, Castle Cove, Crows Nest*, Chatswood, Chatswood West, Lane Cove North, Middle Cove, Naremburn, Neutral Bay*, Northbridge, North Cremorne, North Sydney*, Roseville*, St Leonards* and Willoughby. In the 2019 elections, Gladys won the seat with 27,292 votes (57%); Labor's Justin Reiss won 6,875, and Daniel Keogh (Greens) won 5,342.

Fairly homogenous, comfortably middle class (not counting any Greens hidden in the bushes), with a well stocked Dan Murphy's, a rather dull Penshurst St post office, in contrast to the stylish black & red themed Wyllie's martial arts gym across the road, where Margaret Cunneen SC gets her boxing gloves on, and her grown up sons train customers in martial arts, as does her husband Greg. More of an opera and books consumer, Gladys is not a customer.

The iconic Willoughby Hotel, on the corner of Penshurst and McMahon streets, first drew beer in 1899. The three storey building operates three bars and a bistro, function facilities and a covered beer garden. After some negative patron reviews a few years ago, the pub has made huge strides and now earns praise from 2021 customers, for example: "marvellous" wrote one in June, "consistently good food ... the upstairs dining area is a good option" noted another in April. Not that Gladys was likely to pop in. Her electoral office was three kms away, in Sailors Bay Road, Northbridge, a shop in a modern commercial/apartment building, in total contrast to the old pub. But the large Armenian community in Willoughby and adjacent Chatswood is close to that old pub – the Armenian community centre is two blocks away along Penshurst Street. In 2015, Willoughby Council passed a motion recognising 'the genocide of Armenian, Greek and Assyrian peoples by the then Ottoman Government between 1915 and 1922 and condemns these acts...'

It was at a Christmas 2021 function at the Willoughby Hotel where a few locals told me how Gladys was loved by her community – right or wrong. They weren't Armenian, either.

On another occasion, down the road at the Bridgeview Hotel, I was introduced to a small group of Armenians who also sang her praises. Sitting around a table in the rooftop terrace, they were relaxed in Aussie pub mode. One couple – he Armenian, she Australian - had met by chance in Byron Bay on separate holidays, after having previously met a couple of times, while she was a youngster working at McDonalds. Their daughter was arranging a group photo...

A bald chap with a friendly face bought a round but had to go soon, to switch places with his brother around the corner, looking after their ailing mum suffering from dementia.

When the conversation turned to Gladys, it became clear she is regarded as something of a local hero.

She was always top of the class at school, says one local businessman man who went to the Armenian school with her on Saturdays. He remembers she spoke 'correct' Armenian, not the casual slang he was using. She was regarded as intelligent without being bookish or nerdy, and nobody was surprised that she grew up to handle responsible jobs before entering parliament.

Like all young Armenian women, says the businessman, she was a private young woman. There was nothing unusual in her keeping any male friends away from her parents and siblings. That is the norm, and jumping to culturally misguided conclusions about that aspect is dismissed as ignorant. (A slap in the face for the ICAC questioning about her then boyfriend...)

But she would connect easily enough with people on a day to day level.

The words most used to describe her personally are warm, friendly, unaffected, pleasant and bright. There had never been any negative stories about her in the suburb, and her treatment at the ICAC offended the entire Armenian community. Far from doing anything that could be called corrupt, Berejiklian was seen as a committed politician, keen to serve her electorate and the State.

These people were outraged at what they saw as the ICAC's ignorant, nasty and unwarranted investigation of their heroine. They scoffed at the idea she would do anything 'corrupt'. And they insist it isn't just an 'Armenian solidarity thing'.

It seems that her personal standing in her electorate – and in the state generally - was always positive. Her political profile shows that as Treasurer (2015 – 2017), Gladys oversaw the New South Wales budget return to surplus. This was the first time New South Wales had been declared debt-free in more than 20 years. She also oversaw the part-privatisation of the state's electricity network.

But some of her decisions as Transport Minister (April 2011- April 2015) drew criticism, notably about ferry and rail purchases that delivered inferior products with problems.

And as Premier, in October 2018, Gladys gave permission for advertising to be projected on the sails of the Sydney Opera House for The Everest Stakes (thoroughbred horse race), drawing widespread condemnation and criticism from many in the community, with a poll declaring that 80% of respondents opposed this decision.

It was the strength of her personal standing that carried through to her state and national acclaim in handling the management of Covid 19. This was despite some excessively restricting advice such as that only one person is allowed to leave their home for shopping, browsing is not allowed and to think about leaving home or "can I get it online". "Browsing, killing time, is not a good enough reason to leave your house," she reminded the millions of Aussies currently in lockdown. It wasn't a message universally well received ...

Perhaps the biggest black mark of her Premiership came in July 2021, when in an overly cautious decision Gladys closed down the construction industry across Greater Sydney. The most egregious part of the decision was that it was made without the imprimatur of medical advice. On July 21, 2021, The Daily Telegraph ran an 'individual example' story about Luke Caridi, general manager of major building supplier Sand4U at Sefton, who said he had been forced to put the majority of his 24 staff on paid and unpaid leave after the business drastically cut its operating hours. "We're just trying to make the best of a difficult situation," he said.

"I'm stressed, but I'm more stressed for my staff — it's not just the financial side, it's the mental side. These people are used to turning up for work and now they don't have that."

While Sand4U usually ships out 1000 tonnes of building supplies a week, it was now doing "20 to 30 cubic metres of garden mix" as it ran a skeleton crew to cater for emergency construction stocks."

The Sydney Morning Herald (July 18, 2021) had reported that the shutdown would affect more than a quarter of a million workers and deliver a $1.4 billion blow to the NSW economy.

Gladys had previously drawn heavy criticism from One Nation NSW Leader, Mark Latham (no relation to former ICAC Commissioner Megan Latham) in 2019 over a proposed abortion Bill. Writing in *The Australian* (August 20, 2019), Andrew Clennell (not a Gladys fan, either) reported:

"One Nation leader Mark Latham has delivered a stunning attack against Premier Gladys Berejiklian during debate on the abortion bill in the upper house, accusing her of "betraying the parliament and people of NSW" by supporting the bill decriminalising abortion and labelling her "dictatorial".

"Ms Berejiklian backed down yesterday and her government moved that the abortion bill did not have to be resolved this week, with debate to occur

today and tomorrow and amendments to be moved in the upper house in three weeks' time.

"But as debate went on, and with thousands protesting against the bill outside parliament in Martin Place tonight, Mr Latham accused Ms Berejiklian of operating with a left-wing cross-party cabal.

"With some fanfare after the March election, the Premier said she wanted to 'modernise' the NSW Parliament," Mr Latham said.

"Instead, she has taken us back to the dark ages."

Latham was up and running; he continued:

"A Premier who discarded government business in the Legislative Assembly and made scores of hours of debate available for a private members' bill introduced by the Green-left Independent Member for Sydney, Alex Greenwich.

"One member in one seat who won 18,000 votes at the last election — that is, less than 0.3% of the people of the state of NSW.

"But that's the Berejiklian-Greenwich Government for you: minority interests, with a minority agenda, using backdoor means to try to dominate the majority.

"I campaigned for four months for State Parliament and no one in the electorate advocated for an abortion bill.

"Hundreds of other issues were seen as more important.

"This was to have been an ambush whereby the lower house would debate and pass the abortion bill in one week and the Legislative Council would do the same the following week.

"What we are witnessing here is a weakening of the traditional two-party system, where power in this place does not necessarily rest in the Liberal Party or the Labor Party, but has been co-opted and controlled by a secretive, cross-party cabal.

"It's more evidence of the march through institutions, especially in the National Party.

"Once social conservatives, some of its members are now greener than the Greens."

A reader commenting on the article under the handle, Crocodylus pontifex, wrote: "Mark Latham - a man who would rather have a fight than a feed. Always has been, always will be. He'd join any party that indulges his appetite for a blue. This week it's One Nation; next week it could be the Chinese Communists. He doesn't care - just bring on the biff!"

But another, 'Jon', replied: "IMHO Mark Latham has always been a straight shooter, calling a spade a spade, One Nation is only a platform for him to expose hypocrisy in politics, been there done that. You see what you get with Mark Latham, he is only telling the truth and the hypocrite bedwetters hate it to be exposed."

Gladys has had her share of critics, of course, and the abortion bill was an opportunity for many of those to vent their anger. People are complex, often contradictory in some ways and Gladys is no different. She elicits praise and condemnation as all politicians do; she is seen by her colleagues through a different lens to that of her political opponents or the arms-length public, not to mention her Armenian community.

Liberal Party Federal Vice President Teena McQueen has known Gladys for years, through the Liberal Party. How does she see her?

"Oh, she's an inspiration to women. You know, what she's done. For her community and her party. She has a cast iron character. Her outstanding characteristic is loyalty and I mean that's quite rare in politics."

Would Teena say that Gladys might have made a mistake in not talking about her then boyfriend Daryl? "I think I would. I think that was my greatest disappointment in her because I think it was unfair to her colleagues, at least not to confide in her chief of staff or colleagues. I can understand why she didn't, but I think it, you know, it could have compromised the whole government. You know the ministry..."

Teena McQueen understands why. "I think she was incredibly torn to do that. I think she wasn't certain of Daryl's commitment to her, so she didn't really want to, you know, confide in people, but at the same time, I think, it was serious enough that she should have given a couple of people a heads up."

Could Gladys ever return to politics? "She would not want to return to politics and I don't think she could. I knew when the Prime Minister was tapping around for her to stand but she had no intentions of standing."

What does she make of Peter van Onselen's gossipy revelations of text messages deriding the Prime Minister and calling him not interested in people, a 'horrible, horrible person,' and a 'psycho', between Gladys and an unnamed cabinet minister at the National Press Club (February 1, 2022)?

"He's trying to distract from a problem with someone who has made abuse allegations against him at work. He (PvO) did that successfully, but I think that's a dog act … you know, they're historical texts, not current, and I think the best of us say things in a moment of rage. We've all done it. You know, so I think it was dreadful thing to do to a former premier. Just a low act by PvO.

"I've said things in a spot where I'm really frustrated and text a friend over the Prime Minister. I mean, I haven't meant it. Yeah, it's just … you just express frustration. That's very common in politics. You know, very common, yes, and in life generally. But we love [the PM] dearly…"

GLADYS THROUGH THE LENS & PENS OF THE MEDIA

By the start of the new year, talk (or gossip) of a new job for Gladys was providing headlines, if not actual news. On February 6, 2022, *The Sunday Telegraph*'s Linda Silmalis opened her The Sauce column with a bit of speculation under the confident headline, "New man, new job". New man was a bit out of date (the column said 'it was still going strong') and new job was a rumour, but then The Sauce is not The Steak…

"SHE got her love life back on track after ditching dodgy Daryl – now there is talk that former premier Gladys Berejiklian is on the cusp of launching her new career. The gossip among Willoughby locals helping Ms Berejiklian's replacement Tim James campaign ahead of next Saturday's byelection was that their former member had snared a new job. One source close to the former Willoughby MP would only confirm that the exbanker had been "inundated" with offers. However, the source would not reveal if she had accepted any. "If you say the talk among locals is that she has a new job, you'll be fine," the source helpfully advised.

"However, another well connected senior Liberal in Willoughby last week claimed that matters were far more progressed with Ms Berejiklian in "advanced talks" with her future employer. As for what the job might be, the source noted the former premier's close friendship with Macquarie Bank ex-chairman Kevin McCann. Could she be following in the footsteps of former premiers Mike Baird and Bob Carr with a job at the 'millionaire factory'? When we approached a member of Ms Berejiklian inner-circle to obtain a comment, it was a case of, 'if you don't hear from me …' As for her love life, we can confirm the relationship between Ms Berejiklian and high-

profile barrister and Eels tragic, Arthur Moses, is still going strong with the pair recently attending dinner with friends. Meanwhile, The Sauce has also been told that Daryl, the disgraced Wagga Wagga MP, may have a new love interest. Stay tuned."

***

Not all politicians are treated like movie stars in the media. Just a few get a make over for a glam photo shoot to illustrate a major profile about them in *The Australian Women's Weekly.* The fusion of fame with politics is reserved for those who resonate with the public. In a cynical view, the decision to feature a politician usually means that commercial considerations have determined that the subject will help drive sales. In other words, the public's stamp of approval begets the fashion shoot…sort of thing. Gladys was clearly 'in fashion' in early 2021.

The headline over Penelope Pelecas' April 22, 2021 story trumpeted *mamamia*'s coverage of the AWW coverage…

"Laidback Gladys Berejiklian almost unrecognisable in new magazine shoot

We're use (sic) to seeing the New South Wales premier in structured, conservative clothing, often in hues of black, grey and navy, however, Gladys Berejiklian is almost unrecognisable in a new magazine shoot with The Australian Women's Weekly.

The lifestyle magazine shared images from the laidback photoshoot, which feature in the latest edition of the magazine out this week, on its Instagram account on Thursday. The premier can be seen posing in a beautiful striped blue off-the-shoulder maxi dress, cinched in at the waist.

According to the Daily Mail, the gorgeous dress is designed by Aussie fashion label Carla Zampatti. The look was completed with a pair of nude slip-on flats, adding a flair of effortlessness to the ensemble, while Gladys's hair was styled in soft waves. It's not clear where the photo was taken, and whether it was in fact Gladys' home in Sydney, but the premier appears to be posing in a stunning outdoor area.

Fans were impressed with the photoshoot, with one commenting: "Beautiful and strong woman. I admire her. Love her dress and the natural photo." Another simply stated: "Love this woman." While a third said: "So much respect and admiration for this great premier. Love her dress and she's looking beautiful."

In the accompanying interview the premier opened up about the drama surrounding her personal relationship with former MP Daryl Maguire. In October 2020, it was revealed that the pair had a relationship for a number of years, a fact Gladys later confirmed. However, at the time, the premier's former flame was under investigation for allegedly using his position in parliament to further his business interests, which you could imagine did not sit well with Gladys' critics and led to calls for her to step down as premier.

Now speaking to the The Australian Women's Weekly, Gladys revealed neither her parents, or her sisters, "with whom she is close", knew about her relationship with the former MP, something, she says, she now regrets.

"I couldn't," she said. "I wasn't allowed. There was a process in place ... I just knew I had to deal with it myself."

The premier also spoke about how it felt to have her privacy invaded, saying: "But that's the thing about public life. Even if you're a very private person, which I am — I'm still very private - even so, there's nothing about you that's off limits, unfortunately. Sometimes it verges on disrespect, but that's just the way it is and you have to accept that."

***

In *The Weekly*, Samantha Trenoweth reports about a visit by the NSW Premier with then NSW Rural Fire Service Commissioner Shane

Fitzsimmons. to a community just south of Bateman's Bay during the "hideous black summer" of 2019-20.

"As we were leaving," the former NSW Rural Fire Service Commissioner recalls, "a lady came up to the Premier and said, 'We've got no communication here and I have family who will be worried about me,' and while she was speaking, others standing around said that they were in the same situation too."

So Gladys collected their phone numbers, and "as soon as we got back into mobile range, there she was in the back seat of the car and you could hear her on the phone: 'Oh hello, it's Gladys Berejiklian here. Yes, I am the Premier, but I've just been with such-and-such and they wanted me to give you a call and let you know that they're doing okay.'"

Shane chuckles with genuine affection. It was a classic Gladys moment – calling into play the winning combination of diligence and concern that earned her the trust of the state during that terrifying fire season and then the pandemic.

"There were," Gladys says with characteristic understatement, "a lot of difficult days that summer," driving up and down the coast, looking trauma in the eye, sweating on the lives of firefighters, farmers, people in blazing towns.

"There would be times when Commissioner Fitzsimmons would let me know that there were fire crews missing or people in houses who weren't accounted for," she remembers. "There were some frightening moments. The first day of the year was confronting. Commissioner Fitzsimmons and I went to Malua Bay and there were people who had fled for their lives just hours before and gone to the evacuation centre. It was chaotic."

Then there was the rebuild, which is immense and ongoing. It will, Gladys says, take years. She recently visited fire-affected communities again, more than a year on, and says that "for those people who have been impacted, it's still very real, very raw. It's like losing a loved one – everyone else moves on and you're still grieving."

Gladys will never forget a certain date: January 25 last year.

The smoke had barely cleared from the summer's firestorms – in some places it hadn't – when Australia's first case of COVID-19 was confirmed in Victoria. Again, the level-headed Premier rallied. She put a crisis team in place because "as horrible as the bushfires were," she says, "they'd taught me the importance of having a whole-of-government response.'"

Those were testing times. Initially, fears the virus would take hold as fiercely as it had in Europe looked set to be realised. The Ruby Princess was inexplicably allowed to dock in Sydney Harbour and release its passengers on March 19 – an event ultimately linked to almost 900 cases of COVID-19 and 28 deaths.

Then COVID ran rampant through NSW nursing homes, killing 28 elderly residents – it was nothing like Victoria's 655 aged care deaths, but it was heartbreaking for the families involved, as was the separation of the elderly from their families during lockdown.

During the statewide lockdown, Gladys fronted the cameras daily. Small, wiry, wide-eyed and determined, even when she had bad news to deliver, she gave the impression that the state was in safe hands. She knew that every decision she made would be critical but she didn't flinch, and at the end of the day, her own conscience was her toughest critic.

"I made a decision to say: this is life and death; I don't really care what people think; I'm just going to do what I know is right … Everybody has an opinion, everyone is telling you how to do your job. I knew the people I could trust and should take advice from, and I thought, 'The buck stops with me' … You know the saying, dance like nobody's watching? I wanted to lead like nobody was watching. I didn't want to look back and regret any decision I'd made based on fear or what people might say."

Behind the scenes, Gladys had personal worries too: for friends and family living in Armenia who'd contracted the virus, and for her mother, Arsha, who is 81, and her father Krikor, 88.

"I didn't see them for weeks. I didn't hug them until recently. It was a year without any physical contact," she says, which must have cut deep, not only for them but for Gladys, who lives alone. "I visited them in the driveway and they were in the kitchen. I remember spending Easter by myself, which I'd never done because we do a lot of religious things and it's a very important time for my extended family. I worried about my parents every single day."

The Weekly also broached politics:

"The Greens revealed that more than 95 per cent of the NSW government's $252 million Stronger Communities grants scheme had been allocated to councils in Coalition seats. About which Gladys, who could not be faulted for her candour, admitted that "all governments and all oppositions make commitments to the community in order to curry favour ... The term pork barrelling is common parlance."

Greens MLC David Shoebridge replied: "If this is politics as usual, then the Greens fundamentally believe politics needs a deep, deep clean-out." And observers questioned the Premier's fitness for leadership if this was the type of behaviour to which she was prepared to turn a blind eye.

The Weekly asks Gladys now whether the fact that "pork barrelling" is common practice makes it acceptable. She hesitates and we put it another way: is it fair to give greater benefits to people who vote for you, or who you'd like to vote for you, than to people who need and deserve them?

"Absolutely not," Gladys responds vehemently. "But I also feel you need to be honest with the public on how things do and don't work. Because that's the only way you're going to get real change. I don't know any political party that doesn't make promises at elections. Whether we like it or not, it's part of the system."

Stacking the odds in a grants scheme and making an election promise are not necessarily the same thing – or they shouldn't be. And Gladys at last admits that more protocols could be put in place to ensure taxpayers' money isn't used unfairly to sweeten up voters. But the political roller-coaster didn't end there.

In the midst of the recent allegations of sexual harassment in federal parliament, a former NSW state government staffer, Dhanya Mani, revealed that she had complained twice to the Premier's office of alleged sexual harassment and assault by a parliamentary co-worker, but that there had been no significant investigation, nor support for her personal recovery.

While Gladys has not responded to Dhanya's specific allegations, she has set former minister Pru Goward to work on an inquiry into the state parliament's complaints processes.

And she tells The Weekly: "I commend these brave women for coming forward and telling their stories. People in every walk of life should be thinking, 'Is my workplace a safe place?' And if at times it fails employees, are the processes there to protect people?"

It is testament to the quite extraordinary trust Gladys had built with her constituents through the bushfires and COVID that these snowballing scandals made chinks in her armour but didn't land a body blow. In fact, the most recent NSW polling gives the Premier a 75 per cent approval rating.

It has been a harrowing 18 months but today, sitting outside in the autumn sunshine, watching her sisters chatter and prepare for The Weekly's photo shoot, Gladys has the space to reflect on all she's learned. COVID, for instance, taught her that she's rational, almost to a fault.

"You go through testing times in your life, but it's clearly not on public display the way it has been," she begins. "I know now that I'm more rational than emotional. I've got both. I've got the empathy and compassion, but when everything hits the fan, I'm quite a clear thinker, which you don't know until you're tested, right?"

Gladys has also learnt that there are people in her life who she can count on. Who, we ask, would she ring if she was having a tough time?

"I tend not to ring anyone," she confesses. "I tend to process a lot of things myself."

And who would ring her?

"Lots of people," she laughs, "but that's my nature. I've always been like that. I've always been the one people ring to help them through, and I don't mind. That's just the way I am. I've discovered I'm quite a strong and resilient person. When you really get tested, you realise what kind of person you are."

This past year, however, through some of her toughest days, Gladys says she has "never felt unsupported. My parents, my sisters, my extended family, my close friends were there for me. Professionals and colleagues in the public service supported me, too … And whenever I'm going through a difficult time, the response from the public is phenomenal. I get people sending me gifts and things they've made, and beautiful cards. I'm fortunate that, in my job, I get to see the worst of circumstances, but the best in people. That heartens me … So I never feel alone, I never feel isolated, I never feel woe is me – never ever."

Her sisters have pondered publicly whether she never feels alone because she is a surviving twin – her twin sister was stillborn. Gladys acknowledges there's an impact, but believes it's more of a driver: "I do feel you have a pang of survivor guilt, so you have to justify your existence a bit more."

***

On March 21, 2019, two years before the multi-textured but basically positive *AWW* spread, *mamamia*'s Gemma Bath sought to look 'behind the veil of Gladys Berejiklian 'the politician'. As Gladys told Bath in this interview, "I think it's important for the public to know what makes someone tick. I think it goes with having the so-called top job, it's important to know what my life experience is, and what I bring to the role."

At face value, that sentiment is somewhat at odds with wanting to retain privacy, but it makes sense to Gladys as long as her private, emotional life is kept behind a veil. Bath's article covers what is by now familiar ground, including what must have been added in late 2020, regarding Maguire. This is how it was presented:

"As the Premier of NSW, Gladys Berejiklian has earned a reputation for being private, professional and exceptionally hardworking.

It's a stereotype that some use against her; those who want her to be less guarded, and more open.

Throughout her political career, Berejiklian has never shared details about her relationships or partners, until she disclosed details of her relationship with former colleague Daryl Macguire in October 2020.

The NSW Premier said she was in a "close personal relationship" with the former member for Wagga Wagga at the Independent Commission Against Corruption (ICAC) inquiry, which is currently investigating whether Maguire used his position for personal gain.

Berejiklian said the relationship began in 2015 and finished a few months ago, explaining it wasn't common knowledge in politics because she is a "very private person".

Speaking to Mamamia in 2019, Berejiklian said she made a conscious decision early in her political career to maintain her privacy.

"I've seen phenomenal women on both sides of politics come before me, and no one is focusing on their policies and what they did," she said. "I just made a conscious decision – I watched that, I watched these other women and what these other leaders went through.

"I'd rather be regarded as boring or a workaholic rather than detracting from my role. Because I am not embarrassed to say, I do a good job and I do it a lot better than a lot of men would."

It's been one of her opponents' favourite things to poke holes in, even some colleagues have called her reluctance to talk about her private life a 'weakness'.

"I think it's important for the public to know what makes someone tick. I think it goes with having the so-called top job," she admitted. "It's important to know what my life experience is, and what I bring to the role."

Premier Berejiklian's history is astounding. Her family were victims of the Armenian genocide in 1915, all four of her grandparents were orphaned.

Her parents moved separately to Australia where they married and had three daughters. A young Gladys couldn't even speak English when she started Kindergarten, her parents spoke Armenian at home to preserve their heritage.

Reading her history - you can understand where she got her resilience.

"They taught us [my parents] every day to remember how lucky we are and not to take a single thing for granted. And to most importantly give back and be involved in the community.

"I always say to myself if it's not life or death don't sweat. Everything has a solution," she explained.

This resilience and drive is further fuelled by the fact she had a twin sister, who didn't survive childbirth. Just another reason for Gladys to seize every day, and push herself to make the most of her life. Ms Berejiklian only agreed to tell this story recently, if her mother Arsha volunteered it in an interview, which she did quite willingly.

Gladys found out about her twin when she needed to get her birth certificate for a passport when she was 13. On it it read 'elder of twins.'

"People around me said, you'll never get into politics, you're the wrong surname, wrong gender, wrong this, wrong that. I didn't have one positive thing going for me. But I had this inner confidence to know I wanted to make a difference. Even those close to me were worried about me but I knew I was capable and wanted it," she told Mamamia.

It's this self confidence and tough skin that's helped Ms Berejiklian rise the ranks of a particularly tricky professional ladder. One where you're constantly on display and always being judged.

She hates the fact that female has to come before Premier, and that her gender is a constant source of conversation.

"When I visit schools the boys and girls think nothing of getting a male or female Premier. They're from a different generation. I want them to grow up continuing to have those views. That won't happen if we still make it a novelty when a woman gets to a senior position," she said.

She thinks Me Too helped get overt sexism out in the open, but it's the covert and unconscious bias that she thinks has a long way to go.

When it comes to the idea of balance and that 'women can have it all', Ms Berejiklian laughs.

"I don't think a day goes by where you aren't thinking about stuff like that and for me I have also learnt – people might say why did you choose to do this or choose to do that. Sometimes you don't have a choice," she reasoned.

Berejiklian has never been married and doesn't have children (although she does have six godchildren) but it's something that she finds women are curious about.

"I think if an opportunity comes up you grab it. If something happens and you need to make a decision, make it. Had I met the right person? Of course I would be married. But that doesn't happen for everyone at the right time.

"People are interested I get it, but people shouldn't make assumptions about what decisions women make or don't make. It might not be because they haven't tried, or don't want to, it's just happened this way."

It's something Ms Berejiklian used to wonder about when she was younger. "I wanted to know women's experiences. So you can somehow confirm or change your view – I get it (people's interest)."

For now, as Premier, balance is non existent. Ms Berejiklian loves opera, reading a good book, and enjoying a glass of wine like the rest of us after a big day. But she's very aware that right now, she's married to the job. She's perfectly happy with that.

As for the constant stream of critics, and the criticism within her own head, she has a very clear mindset.

"Never change who you are, people can take it or leave it. Don't feel you've got to conform, don't feel you've got to wear the latest trend. Don't feel you've got to keep up with things. Just live your life honestly.

"There's so much pressure to be a certain way, or look a certain way, to act a certain way and have things done by a certain age... just do what's right for you."

As for being a woman in politics Ms Berejiklian hopes in the future, gender isn't even a consideration.

"Hopefully in the future it'll be normal. Breaking through the novelty, hopefully normalises it," said the Premier.

***

Gladys Berejiklian was invited to participate in this book but politely declined.